SOLUTIONS AMERICA

SOLUTIONS AMERICA

John Ndege

ISBN: 978-1-956074-19-2 (Paperback Edition)
ISBN: 978-1-956074-20-8 (Hardcover Edition)
ISBN: 978-1-956074-18-5 (E-book Edition)

Book Ordering Information

Phone Number: 315 288-7939 ext. 1000 or 347-901-4920
Email: info@globalsummithouse.com
Global Summit House
www.globalsummithouse.com

Printed in the United States of America

CONTENTS

CHAPTER 8

CHAPTER 9

CHAPTER 10

ACKNOWLEDGEMENTS

I would like to thank all people who helped me to make the writing of this book possible. This involved discussing, researching, typing and editing drafts along the way. These also include those who contributed to the cost of printing and marketing of this book.

I would first of all mention my wife Hope and the children Chocho, Dege, Bogo, Pewit, Pochino and Mumu. Friends and relatives who include the following Moses Likwases, Susan Matama, Gladys Kebut, Mike, Isaac, John and Conchita , Nancy Kamau, David Yano Singei, Margaret, Mellisa Kaijuka.

I wish to also acknowledge Global Summit House for republishing the Book especially the following amongst others whom I have come to deal with in the course of republishing the Book namely, Riley Miles, Yvonne Johnson, Henry Thompson, Alice Evans, Mia Tyler, Liv Miller, Phil Ramos, Neil Walker, Missy Charles

They were all Professional and fast in doing their work.

CHAPTER 1

1. SCOPE

(a) I am going to look at the past achievements, failures, the present problems facing USA, and future options and solutions which will help America launch itself into a prosperous future. Among the main topics, I am going to research, discuss, give opinions and suggest solutions are the USA political history including the political party structure, the constitution, and three branches of government. I will be looking at their achievements failures and possible solutions.

(b) I shall also analyze the weaknesses that have developed over time in the free market capitalist system and suggest possible solutions to what was once acknowledged to be but it still is known as the number one envy of the world. It is a system that has encouraged so many people to try to come to the USA and participate in every way possible so that they can also realize their vision of the American dream. The USA is known to have been built mainly by immigrants from all over the world, and that is why it is called and known as the country of immigrants.

(c) I am also going to highlight the main long outstanding unsolved social, economic, and political issues that I believe must be tackled and resolved as a matter of urgency. These are the issues that the American people have, in vain, been expecting their political leaders to find solutions in a way that is beneficial for them and the country. The problems still hanging are many and they are in need of urgent attention if America is to retain its number one position now and in the future. These issues are affecting the economic and social welfare of the people and if left unsolved there is no way that America can continue to lead the world. These issues can only be successfully resolved in a partisan manner because neither party has all the comprehensive answers to these long outstanding problems. These problems have encouraged more and more voters to switch to and from one party to the other and some now define themselves as independents because neither of the two parties has the courage and take the bold step of taking pro-American solutions to their problems. No one can therefore rule out the emergence of a strong third party and if this happened it would drastically change the USA political scene for some time to come. The idea of the USA being and remaining the leader of the free-market world is being compromised and undermined for as long as these issues remain unsolved. Many people believe that leaving these problems unsolved could have been one of the issues which were responsible for the 2007 housing and economic meltdown.

(d) At this juncture I would like to mention some of these pending issues that I have been mentioning. These items among others include problems relating to Medicaid, Medicare, the 2010 healthcare act, social security, energy policy, comprehensive immigration reform, the USA political party structure including the voting system, social problems such as the definition of marriage that is not so well defined and predictable foreign policy. These are some of the urgent and vital problems which must be tackled right away partly by the executive but more so by congress. Congress should adopt a non-partisan and pro-American approach so that solutions can be found so that other equally related important issues such as the budget shortfalls, tax reform, and the national debt can also then be successfully addressed.

(e) On top of the above, I am also going to look at the recent events which have impacted the USA in various ways. These include the following;

(i) The 2001 September 11 attack on the USA and what followed thereafter.

(ii) The 2007 housing bubble and economic meltdown culminated in the worst recession since World War II.

(iii) I'm also including mention of the unexpected natural and unnatural occurrences but with particular reference to Katrina because it exposed glaring weaknesses in the way the capitalist free market system is being implemented. This system was once acknowledged to be the best and the most efficient in the world. The system was let down by too much bureaucracy which lacked quick and fast decision-making decisions and procedures.

There is a growing tendency of running a private capitalist system mixed with too many government restrictions and micro-managing policies at all levels of government. This leads to inefficiency and unfair blame on the free market system when the results do not turn out as efficiently as should be expected. In the case of Katrina, the federal and state governments, Federal Emergency Management Agency (FEMA), and other relevant agencies appear to have underestimated the magnitude of the task before them. They did not take enough precautions or make adequate preparations for the impending disaster from Mother Nature. The residents of New Orleans, Mississippi, and surrounding areas were overnight almost reduced to third world status. Furthermore the people were disappointed by the mismanagement of the funds which Congress and other donors voted to handle situation.

These situations like Katrina should be run by private agencies with logistical support from the concerned government department. The private agencies should form a coordinated system to run these emergencies which need quick action because they are time-sensitive.

My experience in emergency response is that privately run agencies such as Red Cross can respond within about 48 hours to a problem. On the other hand, government-run organizations such as World Food Programme (WFP), FEMA, etc can take days or weeks to respond to urgent emergencies because of the bureaucratic procedures they have to go through. WFP has to get permission from Rome and for other government agencies, they would even take weeks because they have to follow standing procurement procedures. Since emergencies are time-sensitive it is clear that private agencies such as NGOs, churches, etc do the response job most efficiently. They are more likely to give better value for the money utilized in such cases.

CHAPTER 2

DETAILS

2 (A) POLITICAL HISTORY OF USA

The best way, to begin with, is to discuss the political history of the USA. The first thing we shall look at is the declaration of independence and the constitution. Since the two are the main pillars of democracy in the USA.

2 (B) THE DECLARATION OF INDEPENDENCE.

This is one of the landmarks in USA political history. The declaration of independence states that we hold these truths to be self-evident that all men are created equal, that they are endowed by the Creator with certain unalienable rights that among these are life, liberty, and the pursuit of happiness. It goes on to say that whenever any government becomes destructive of these ends, it is the right of the people to alter or abolish it.

It is therefore clear that government should be for the people and by the people and not vice versa. Governments that do not hold regular free and fair elections which reflect the free will of their people must be resisted by the people and world community. This is the only way to ensure that the fundamental rights and freedoms as mentioned in the declaration of independence can be seen to be respected and guaranteed. In the USA these rights are usually taken for granted because they are there.

Although in the USA the electoral system still needs some adjustments, as was clearly experienced during the 2000 presidential elections, the election results which are usually declared reflect the will of the people. There are systems put in place to challenge any shortcomings or abuse of the electoral system. Many other developed countries, especially those in the Western World, also generally adhere to the principles of the free will of the people's choices, and the election results also generally reflect the will of the people.

It is however regrettable to note that there are many people in many other countries who are still struggling and waiting for the opportunity to enjoy these natural rights and freedoms which nobody should beg or fight for. They are still struggling to have their right to decide their political system and leadership choices which must be respected by their political systems. For instance in many countries especially the far-left socialist-leaning countries such as Cuba and North Korea they hold regular elections but the electoral results do not necessarily reflect the will of the people. There is a tendency for such countries to declare election results with a yes popular vote of 90% plus in favor of the sitting party president or favored candidates. It is usually clear and known that the voting procedures and results were not transparent and did not reflect the will of the people.

There are also autocratic regimes such as Iran, Zimbabwe, Egypt, and Burma which also hold regular elections but they also do not reflect the will of the people. They also have a common factor of rigging elections and announcing the rigged results almost immediately after the polls are closed. During the last elections in Iran for instance, within hours of closing the voting president Mahmoud Ahmadinejad was announced to have won the elections. The voters could not believe the news from the election officials because the counting could not have possibly been completed in such a short time. They immediately challenged the results. They organized protest demonstrations but they were unfortunately ruthlessly crushed by the regime. Nobody will ever forget that girl Neda Agha-Soltan who was mercilessly murdered and will always stand as the symbol of the struggle for free and fair elections for the people of Iran who took the risk and fought for their rights in order to have a government that reflects their will.

In Zimbabwe, the international community had to intervene and negotiate a government of national unity because President Mugabe would not leave his presidential seat without bloodshed even if he knew that he had possibly lost the elections. In Zimbabwe, the politics is reported to be so bad that areas which during the election had not voted for Mugabe were denied food and other supplies which were donated by the international community during the famine period that Zimbabwe was experiencing. It is also alleged that the Zimbabwe regime developed and practiced a scotch earth policy for those areas which did not vote for the ruling party. Many people are alleged to have fled to other areas of the country and others fled to the neighboring countries for fear of reprisals. The only way to clear the issue was to recount the votes in a clear and transparent manner. People do not have to beg for this right.

It's a pity that in this 21st century, the world can allow political leaders to treat their countries and people as if they were their personal property. People who try to resist these regimes are often intimidated, repressed, tortured, denied basic freedoms, respect, and justice. Many of them suffer unfair and painful detentions. These regimes orchestrate incidents against their opponents and manipulate votes in their favor to make it appear as if they have won the popular vote.

One of the longest political fighters is Aung San Suu Kyi of Burma. She spent 15 out of her 21 years of politics in detention fighting for freedom and political rights in Burma. Nelson Mandela spent almost half of his life in prison fighting for political rights and equality for all the people of South Africa. Here in USA Martin Luther King paid with his life trying to fight for equal human rights for the minority communities in the USA. The minorities in the USA had to use everything at their disposal including church venues in their struggle to gain equality. They had to form alliances with other disgruntled people like the environmentalists, communists, equal rights women groups, gays etc. in order to put up a strong group fighting for equal treatment. All these had to form alliances because they were fighting a common enemy of unfair treatment. They were fighting for rights as embedded in the declaration of independence and the constitution. Many people in other countries have paid with their lives fighting for political and other freedoms. In Cambodia for instance, millions lost their lives during the political infighting in the country.

It is therefore important that fundamental rights as mentioned in the declaration of independence are jealously defended by the people of the USA and they do not allow them to slip through their fingers. The loss of these rights normally starts as a joke. The people start losing these rights piece by piece and over time they come to realize that they have lost their rights because they did not challenge the perpetrators. This is usually done in the name of national security concerns. The most sensible solution is putting provisos for bad elements who do not respect the natural rule of justice. The executive always enjoys amassing power so that they can direct and control the lives of the people. This eventually ends in the politics of intimidation and fear instilled in the population. To revert back to the good days of good governance is usually bloody and costly. Because no regime enjoys handing back whatever power they have usurped.

The United Nations Organization should devise a system where they can give an opinion whether any country's election results reflect the will of the people and also whether the election was free and fair. They should also devise scores for the degree of respect for these fundamental freedoms and rights. In this way, at a glance people can assess how democratic these countries are. This would be a great contribution to world peace and democracy and should be endorsed by all the UN members.

2 (C) THE US CONSTITUTION

The other landmark was the promulgation of the US constitution which has been operative since September 17th,

1787. The constitution created three branches of a federal type of government namely:

2 c (i) The Legislative Branch. This is the bicameral branch known as congress. It has the House of Representatives who represent the people and the senate whose members represent the people in those states. The two houses are co-equal and it requires both of them to accent to a bill before it can be sent to the president to be signed into law. Congress makes laws and all legislative power is vested in it.

2 c (ii) The Executive Branch. This branch enforces the laws and is lead by the president. There is a vice president, secretaries, and other state servants of some of whom require Senate approval. The president also enjoys among other federal executive powers as the commander in chief of all federal armed forces.

2 c (iii) The Judiciary Branch. This branch is headed by The Supreme Court. The Supreme Court and the lower federal and state courts interpret the law.

2 c (iv) Separation of Powers. In order to avoid as much conflict as possible between the above three branches of government, the constitution clearly spells out their separate scope roles and functions. The main idea was that one powerful branch does not expand at the expense of the other two. It is therefore important in order to maintain this balance, that decisions made by one branch in accordance with the provisions of the constitution are respected and honored by the other two.

For instance, whatever the judiciary decides should be respected and implemented, and enforced unreservedly by the executive branch, and also respected by congress. What has been happening in many countries USA included is that the executive normally oversteps its powers and tries to undermine the other two branches and this usually undermines the democratic set up creating conflict. It is usually known that there are many instances when the executive can ignore to honor and implement a court order such as releasing a person who the courts have found innocent. The executive either refuses to implement the order or can release the person only to re-arrest the person immediately thereafter. This makes a mockery of democracy and undermines the power of the judiciary.

In other instances, Congress or the Legislature can pass a law retrospectively in order to defeat a court ruling. This again undermines the concept of the rule of law and the independence of the courts. In the worst situation, the army can usurp the powers of the three branches and rule by decree.

All these scenarios are not healthy for democracy to thrive. These are just a few examples of what can undermine the concept of separation of powers of the branches of government. Good governance can only thrive when the different branches of government respect each other as laid down by the provisions of the constitution of the day.

Here in the USA although the constitution is largely respected by the three branches, over the years the three arms of government have tried to gain more power at the expense of each other as we shall expound under.

CHAPTER 3

CONFLICT BETWEEN BRANCHES OF GOVERNMENT

3 (A) CONFLICT AND POWER STRUGGLE WITHIN THE THREE BRANCHES OF GOVERNMENT

3 a (i) The Judiciary: The judiciary seems to be the arm that has managed to maintain its independence and power as provided by the constitution. This is despite the fact that judges of the Supreme Court are appointed by the president and confirmed by the senate. The important thing is that once appointed, the president or congress has no power to fire or direct the functions of the judiciary. Supreme Court judges and other lower-level judges serve until they decide to retire or die in office. They can only be removed from the bench for non-political reasons such as judicial misconduct. Proper procedures for the removal of judges are clearly laid out.

There are however instances when especially, the executive has been critical of the judiciary.

(i) For instance, recently, President G.W. Bush criticized the Supreme Court judges by accusing them of ruling from the bench. He accused them of creating laws instead of interpreting the law in accordance with the constitution. Maybe this is because they made a ruling which was not according to the way the president had wanted.

(ii) President Obama also went on and scolded the Supreme Court judges for their ruling regarding campaign finance issues during his state of the union address to the nation in 2009. The ruling favored no restrictions to campaign spending by corporations, and the president wanted the restrictions to remain as was part of the law. The Supreme Court scoffed off his criticism insisting that they were only interpreting the law and protecting the rights and freedoms of individuals as prescribed in accordance with the provision of the constitution. As a result, his relationship with some of the Supreme Court judges has since been strained. Some of the Supreme Court judges skipped attending the next presidents' address to the nation. Maybe they were trying to send and remind the executive about their independent constitutional role. The executive ought to realize that the justices only interpret the law in accordance with the current law and the constitution. The executive should know better that it is the only congress that is vested with the power of making or changing laws. The judges should not be compelled to administer justice according to the wishes of the executive or congress. If dissatisfied with any ruling congress can change the law, provided that it is in accordance with provisions of the constitution. If any law is suspected to be unconstitutional by anybody, it can only be challenged through the courts and declared so by the lawful courts. Various people, States, groups, etc for instance have challenged the recently passed 2010 health care and reconciliation act because they are of the opinion that some parts of the act are unconstitutional. The matter is now before the Supreme Court which has accepted to hear the matter. The Supreme Court ruling is the final ruling on any judicial issue and whatever they finally decide cannot be challenged but must be implemented, unless subsequently amended by congress in a lawful way.

(iii) There are also other areas of conflict within the judiciary itself. For instance, some people feel that justices and the jury could be influenced when administering justice if they fear that their ruling could throw the country in chaos. In the case of O.J Simpson murder case, for instance, it was felt by some people that if O.J Simpson was found guilty for the murder of his wife, there could have been riots all over the country. This phenomenon they believe could have influenced the way the jury returned their verdict. However, there are no concrete facts to support such an opinion.

(iv) Recently the Attorney General also intimated that some of the 911 suspects would not be released and would remain in detention even if they were found not guilty by the civilian courts. Many people are appalled by this opinion and they believe that such a move would set a bad precedent and would undermine the power of the law and the judiciary. It would also be considered a mockery of the rule of law as it would affect good governance in the following manner:

a) It would make a mockery of the judicial system and powers if the court orders are not respected and defied by the executive.

b) Such a policy might develop into a conflict with other branches of government, and the constitution itself.

c) Such a move would send a bad message to the rest of the world especially the emerging democracies, who are trying to administer justice in accordance with the rules of the law. It would appear to them that the USA does respect their judicial system and so why should they.

d) Such undemocratic measures would be welcomed, by such countries as Iran, Venezuela which do not usually respect the rule of law in their countries and would authenticate their bad policies behavior, and reputation. These countries would use this as an example to justify their actions and would quote the USA so as to prove themselves right. It would be surprising and sad to see that the leader of the free world can contemplate implementing such acts which appear to be in conflict with the rule of law and put the USA in the category of these countries.

CHAPTER 4

4. THE EXECUTIVE

4 (a) The executive has in many ways been more aggressive in attempting to acquire more power at the expense of the other two arms of the government. Lee Hamilton in his article on congress and the president believes that the annual state of the union's address to a joint session of congress sets the tone of the president by highlighting executive priorities and activities for the following year. This event is covered live by all media which includes TV networks, Newspapers, and radios only to mention but a few and debated for days thereafter. Members from both houses with respect give their support to the president. One GOP senator who called President Obama a liar during the state of the union address in 2009 was quickly denounced and forced to apologize. His rights of free expression were not welcome on that night. This, therefore, gives the president a lot of respect and attention because of the wide coverage, and Congress is obliged to honor him for that occasion. The other two branches of government attend the occasion and this opportunity is only given to the president. It, therefore, builds clout for the presidency against the other two branches of government.

There is no doubt that the expansion of the media and the press has given the president more ammunition to surpass the other two branches and especially congress. It is easier for the press and media to cover one person than so many members of congress. The president can also directly contact the people at will through TV coverage and country-wide tours while congress is busy legislating. Maybe that's why the constitution was designed to give more cloud to the congress so that aggressive presidents can be brought into check.

4. (b) It has been observed that over time various presidents have succeeded in making the executive branch more and more powerful. Presidents Theodore Roosevelt and Franklin D Roosevelt succeeded in expanding presidential powers to actively introduce and influence the outcome of legislation bills. Before them, it was congress that was the main driving force. This is one of the ways Presidents have developed in amassing their powers at the expense of mainly congress.

4. (c) Recently during the health care and education reconciliation reform debates, President Barack Obama used every ammunition and tactic he could master to influence the passage of the measure that had failed congress to resolve for many years. He used his office to influence representatives of his party in the house and senate by among other tactics promising favors in return for support of the act. He is also said to have used intimidation tactics by threatening to delay or cut off funding of programs meant for areas of those representatives who were not in support of the bill. Through the Democratic National Congress, he is said to have threatened to use media to expose Democrats and some Republicans in their areas of representation if they were not in support of the bill. It has been said that he together with speakers of both houses of Congress made sure that they pass the 2400 page bill without much scrutiny by the members of congress. Members of the house were told to pass the bill first and then read the details later. Members of the senate were given very little time to read the bill or propose amendments or additions to the bill before the vote to pass the measures was taken.

When things appeared to stall in the Senate, he is said to have made sure that the Speaker and the Democrats use the nuclear option to pass the last contentious parts of the health care and education reconciliation reform bill.

In the end, the bill was passed and signed into law. The Healthcare act however is beginning to haunt many of those members of Congress who passed it without major scrutiny. Some bad provisions of the act are also forcing the government to give exemptions and concessions to such institutions as unions, teachers, and many companies, etc from adhering to certain provisions of the act because if implemented the insurance premiums would be hiked. This move means that the ground is not leveled for everyone and therefore animal farm is in action. Selective application of the law is dangerous and therefore the law must be revised to make it fair for everybody without exception because what is good for the goose is also good for gender.

It is also important to note that a few sitting Senators and Members of the house were enthusiastic about using the Healthcare and Education Reconciliation Act as a campaign tool of success during the November 2010 mid-term election campaigns. Maybe this is because they recognized that 61 percent of the population is still opposed to the Healthcare and Education Reconciliation Act which amended the Patient Protection and Affordable Care Act of 2010.

Matters might get even more complicated as the full impact on the details of the act is fully felt as events unfold during the period up to 2014 when the act kicks in full gear. This is because the public and legislations are yet to understand everything since some of the provisions of the act kick in during 2013 and 2014.

However, this case goes to show that the President has developed a lot of ammunition and clout to influence the outcome of legislation and consequently reduced the power and independence of Congress.

4. (b) The President can also use the veto power to reject bills passed by Congress. Congress however can override the veto with a 2/3 majority. If line by line Veto becomes acceptable, this will further expand the Presidents' options of action on bills passed by congress ready for the president to sign. Allowing the President to cherry-pick on what section of the bills sent to him/ her for signature will definitely further weaken Congress. For a

bill to go the to President's desk, a lot of compromises have been made. It is better for the President to either reject or accept the compromised solution.

4. (e)Usually, the Presidential powers are more pronounced if both Houses of Congress belong to his party, although this is not always plain sailing. This is because in either party some members in congress belong to the extreme left or right of their party while others belong somewhere in between and are commonly known as moderates. Members of Congress also represent different areas whose needs are not uniform. It is not uncommon to find members of Congress from different parties having the same ideas on some issues and what they support might be different from their party positions. All these positions have to be reconciled if common grounds over issues are to be found.

4. (f) Presidents in the recent past have also had the tendency of appointing presidential advisors commonly known as Czars who do not need congressional approval. They are just rewarded for their political support. The power and number of these Czars have been on the increase. Since the Czars are not vetted and confirmed by the Senate, the congressional vetting powers have as a result been sidelined. Recently President Obama appointed Elizabeth Warren to head another agency to oversee the consumer protection agency. Her budget will be funded by the Federal Reserve System in order to avoid blockage of her funds by Congress. Her appointment will not require Senate approval. Congress cannot, therefore, control her activities, since her vote will be provided by the Federal Reserve System.

4. (g) The executive has also increasingly been using administrative means to bypass Congress. For instance, a department dealing with carbon dioxide emissions can declare carbon dioxide a dangerous substance to human beings. They can therefore use this excuse to administratively pass tax measures to address the issue. In this way, the executive can pass the measure concerning carbon emissions and impose taxes although the matter has been blocked by the senate. If Congress keeps quiet then the

measure would have proved that Congress can be by-passed by making laws and policies administratively.

4. (h) The President can also issue executive orders which are binding on federal agencies but do not require congressional approval. All recent Presidents have used these powers more often. Such measures can include recess appointments of people unlikely to get congressional approval.

4. (i) Another measure was the establishment of the office of Legislative Affairs. This was set up to help the President liaise with Congress.

4. (j) Clemency: the President can also use powers to pardon people who are serving sentences. This is another weapon the President can use to gain more clout.

4. (k) Executive privilege is another avenue where the President can withhold information from Congress and the general public. There was conflict when G.W. Bush refused his aides to appear before Congress. His officers had been subpoenaed by Congress but were directed by the President not to appear, sighting executive privilege.

4. (L) CONCLUSION

All in all, the Presidential powers seem to be expanding without much challenge from the other two branches and the general public. This is especially so on the side of Congress as political party positions over issues seem to suppress individual opinions and positions of the Members of Congress.

4. (m) To further illustrate the clout of Presidential powers we shall next look at the recent tenures of the USA Presidents.

POLICIES AND EXECUTIVE DECISION OF RECENT USA PRESIDENTS

Different Presidents have had their successes and failures in different ways. In this section, I am giving a summary of recent presidential tenures to further illustrate how their actions and decisions have affected events and gradually affecting the effectiveness of the other two branches of government especially Congress. Generally, US Presidents who had a vision for American and handled their foreign affairs successfully are some of the most highly rated Presidents today and have influenced politics even up to today.

4(m) (a) I will start by mentioning the tenure of J.F. Kennedy, 1961-1963. He had a vision of taking America on a journey to land a man on the moon. He also challenged Americans by asking them what they can do for their country, other than what their country can do for them. He preached peace and started the Peace Corps to propagate this peace worldwide. This peace mission is still alive today, although its impact on society today is not as much as it was during his time. It seems there is no will to keep the program as was originally intended. The program appears to be more technical and political rather than cultural.   His mission to help Cubans rid themselves of communism failed, but at least he tried with what is known as the failed Bay of Pigs. Kennedy also stood firm when the Russians tried to bring and install nuclear weapons in Cuba in what is commonly known as the Cuban missile crisis. Unfortunately, death robbed him prematurely and we shall never know what the whole story would have been having he lived to complete his term. America however landed a man on the moon and many good things have risen out of this mission. The benefits to science and mankind from this venture have been enormous. These include further exploration of outer space, the science lab and other types of communication satellites, GPS systems, Star Wars, weather satellites, etc. The world stage has definitely changed dramatically as scientific benefits out of outer space technology are being felt and as more research is being developed and existing technologies are improved upon.

(B) LYNDON BAINES JOHNSON, 1963-1969

LBJ succeeded as President after the assassination of John Kennedy. He is widely acknowledged for being able and successful in pushing legislation in Congress.

(C) JIMMY CARTER ERA (1976-1980)

Jimmy Carter was perhaps the most sincere President in the recent past. His soft handling of the Iranian hostage issue however overshadowed many of the good things he did. He, for instance, must be credited for creating the Departments of Energy and Education. He was also instrumental to the success of Camp David's accords between Israel and Egypt. This earned the Sadat and Begin the 1978 Nobel Prize award and the signing of the 1979 Egypt/Israel Peace Treaty. President Carter was also involved with the Salt Talks.

The 444 days the American hostages were held under siege by Iranian students was unacceptable to the public, and this is partly why President Carter lost the 1980 presidential elections to Ronald Reagan. There was drama when the hostages were released within hours after Ronald Reagan assumed office. The sudden release of these hostages must have even surprised the Carter Administration.

However, after leaving office, Jimmy Carter continued to fight for many causes including the encouragement and observance of free and fair elections, especially in the emerging democracies. He emphasized that every vote must count. He also emphasized that voter intimidation and other undemocratic practices such as ghost voters, and other types of vote-stealing, and intimidation of candidates were unacceptable. He deserves respect for this mission but the same principle should also apply in the USA no matter what candidate you support. I was therefore surprised when Jimmy Carter told Hilary Clinton to pull out of the Democratic Party primaries race well before the voting process was over. Maybe he forgot what he was preaching and encouraging everywhere when these matters were concerning elections in the emerging democracies.

His recent comments regarding the situation in the Middle East, especially in connection with the Israeli-Palestinian conflict seemed to indicate that Jimmy Carter wanted Israel to give in too many concessions whereas he was not asking the Palestinians to also equally give in to the same extent. This gave the impression of him being more pro-Palestinian as regards the peace initiatives in the Middle East.

Jimmy Carter also continues to broker for general peace and human rights in the world. It was not surprising that he received the 2002 Nobel Peace Prize even after leaving office. To date, he is the only President to receive this honor while not in the office. He also must be credited with his mission to eradicate the guinea warm all over the world.

(D) RONALD REAGAN ERA 1980-1988

When Ronald Reagan assumed office in 1980, the US had been overtaken by the communist world both economically and militarily. The US and the western world were losing the Cold War. In fact, it was generally accepted that the USA and its allies were the weaker sides in the cold war conflict. The US economy was also facing almost hyperinflation.

Reagan immediately commenced dealing with these problems. Within hours of taking office, the US Embassy hostages were released by the Iranians. Maybe the Iranians knew that Reagan was a no-nonsense man. Reagan skillfully worked with Congress to reduce taxes and government expenditure. These measures helped to reduce inflation, stimulate economic growth and development. Reagan held the view that it is better, while negotiating, to take half a loaf than take nothing.

The same philosophy helped him to negotiate with allies and other foreign leaders. He developed better relationships with the Soviet Union through the policy of détente. Although he was willing to compromise on issues, his main principle policy was to negotiate with what he called peace through strength. His defense budget was the exception in the general reduction of government expenditure. In fact, he increased the defense budget by 35% over the years. There was an arms race between the USA and the Soviet Union, which he commonly described as the evil empire. He could therefore not afford to be complacent because the USA was known to be lagging behind the Soviet Union in military strength by the time Reagan took over the presidency. He started the Star Wars program which frightened the Soviet Union. He restored American dignity and the Americans plus the allies had now started speaking and negotiating from economic clout, military confidence, and strength. This was the beginning of the end of the Cold War. In 1979 Reagan took a bold step and told the Soviet Union to tear down the Berlin Wall. The fall of the Berlin Wall was a clear manifesto that the free world had started taking the upper hand.

Although the Soviet Union disintegrated during the G.H. Bush presidency the background work had been done during the Reagan presidency. In fact, G.H. Bush was Reagan's Vice President.

My personal experience is that I remember having held a conversation with one US diplomat at the USA embassy in Uganda who predicted that the Soviet Union was going to break up because it was created by the use of force, in contrast to the US which was created by treaty. I could not believe him and I told him that he was a dreamer because Russia handled the union allies with an iron fist and therefore his opinion was farfetched. When one thought about what had happened to Hungary in 1956 that kind of idea did not seem feasible. However, it happened and the Soviet Empire was dismantled, thanks to Ronald Reagan. He was a man of vision and determination.

Ronald Reagan dealt with many other issues including making some good decisions for Africa, particularly in the area of economic development. He decided that all emergency aid for Africa should be procured in Africa. This measure stimulated growth for industries producing emergency supply items such as blankets, cooking oil, tents, and agricultural produce such as beans, maize, rice, etc. Almost all the sectors of these economies were booming because of the multiplier effect of these business activities. This went on until the policy was reversed during the Clinton era when the Clinton administration also was trying to sell America and promote American exports. I remember attending a meeting at USAID offices in Kampala between Uganda and the US delegation. At the meeting the USA was urging, Uganda, to buy sugar, cooking oil, etc., from the USA through the Exim Bank. These were items which emerging countries like Uganda, Kenya, and the rest of Africa would have liked to export to the USA because they are primary producers of these products. These are the products that are normally exported by emerging democracies to enable them to earn foreign currencies to pay for their imports.

By the end of his presidency, Reagan had done for America and the free world what no other president had achieved in the recent past. There was peace, social and economic development almost worldwide. The free market concept was now respected as the norm. Socialist countries such as China and Russia were now embracing the concept of the free market system. Today they are now strong economic forces to be reckoned with. They have moved away from the once state-controlled economies towards the free market system.

Even today, Ronald Reagan is the most admired and quoted President by many people and politicians when they want to put their cases across at meetings and gatherings. It seems Reagan is the main reference for excellence for many political leaders struggling for political success. He was regularly quoted by both Republican and Democratic presidential candidates during the 2008 road to the White House campaigns. Many people believe he is the most rated US political executive. The whole world will always admire and respect Ronald Reagan because of his visionary way of leadership. It appears that whatever Ronald Reagan did was for the good and in the best interests of America, the world and not just for his own or that of his party. That I think is one of the secrets of his success.

(E) The G.H.W Bush Era 1989-1992

G.H.W. Bush became President after being the Vice President to Ronald Reagan. He continued with the legacy of what his predecessor had left. In addition, he pledged to make the USA a kinder nation by using the prestige that the nation had gained for the greater good.

Bush saw the Cold War come to an end. He also saw the Soviet communist empire dismantle. The fall of the Berlin Wall was a great symbol of this process. This was one of the fundamental changes the world had ever experienced since the end of the Second World War. It left the USA, the European allies, and the free world with so much respect and power they had not experienced for a long time. The world could now spend less on defense and concentrate on peace, social and economic development. Emerging democracies also went through major social, economic, and political changes. Most of them which had been leaning left such as Tanzania, Kenya, and Uganda started moving and implementing pro-capitalist free-market policies such as privatization and conceding to multi-party democratic political systems. In Africa, immediately after the wave of independence from the colonialists during the '60s and '70s, African leaders developed a new concept of African socialism. President Kwame Nkrumah of Ghana, Patrice Lumumba of Congo, Jaramogi Odinga Oginga of Kenya, Mwalimu Nyerere of Tanzania, Milton Obote of Uganda only to mention but a few, all started the doctrine and implementation of African socialism. This doctrine advocates nationalizing of private industry, services, and property by sharing it among the population so that everybody is equal. They had the belief that if the government-owned the means of producing wealth and guided the economy as it was being done in the soviet union, then they would make everybody rich and happy. This meant the death of such concepts as capitalism and free-market forces. In Uganda, the government started the doctrine of the common man's charter. Under this doctrine, all major industries, banks, and other service industries were nationalized in the name of African socialism. However, the move to the left under the common man's charter was short-lived because his Excellency Milton Obote was overthrown by Iddi Amin Dada. In any case, the people of Uganda had already started resisting the common man's charter and coined it 'common man's shut up. This was because no opinion was allowed to be expressed beyond the concept of the common man's charter. The damage of nationalizing assets had however already been done and it took many years to reverse the effect. Kenya was the only exception where the concept of African socialism did not start from scratch since the then president of Kenya Jomo Kenyatta was a believer in free-market economic policies. Although Kenya has other problems such as government corruption and tribal politics, the private sector in Kenya has developed further than its African neighbors. Kenya has been home to many refugees running away from her neighboring countries because of political conflicts. This is also because Kenya practices a free market system that allows other people to come and invest in the country.

Tanzania for instance had a socialist system called Ujamaa Policy, under the burner of a single party called Chama Cha Mapinduzi. They believed in the utopian concept of people's equality through sharing of the country's resources. For instance, if one had three houses he was encouraged to surrender one house to society for redistribution to those who didn't have one. The government would levy heavy taxes for the second and more houses if the owner did not comply and continued to keep them. The economy had stalled because there was no incentive for the people to struggle and work hard. Those who had resources started buying property and starting a business outside Tanzania because it was taboo to be rich in their own country. All these changes from socialism did not happen overnight but at least there was that move towards the free market system.

These changes were helped by the fact that there was more attention and aid available for these emerging economies. Russia, China, the former Soviet Union partners had also started adopting free-market concepts at differing degrees and as a result, there was less appetite for socialist policies. These moves would see the world's longest economic boom era and genuine peace.

G.H.W. Bush also met some other challenges. Perhaps G.H.W Bush's greatest test was when the Iraqi president Saddam Hussein invaded Kuwait and named it the 19th province. The world led by the USA immediately challenged this provocation. A coalition of over 30 countries under the hospices of the United Nations organized and restored the honor of Kuwait. In the 100 hour Desert Storm ground war that followed 2 months of airstrikes and heavy bombing, the coalition forces led by the USA pushed the Iraqi invaders back into their territory. For some reason, maybe based on Middle Eastern regional politics, Saddam Hussein was left to stay in power. Hussein used this chance to claim that he had actually won the war and chased away the infidels. In fact, many people, especially among many Muslim communities, bought that argument and they believed that Saddam Hussein had actually chased away the coalition forces. In East Africa, this debate lasted for many years. Indeed during the desert storm war, every time Iraq launched a scud missile, there was jubilation, especially among the young and Muslim community. To them therefore the claim was not fiction but real when they were told that Saddam Hussein had actually chased away the coalition forces. Very few of the rural population or even urban areas were looking at CNN or other TV networks to follow the events as they unfolded because such facilities were still being developed and were expensive to install.

It is the opinion of many people that President G.H. Bush miscalculated by not finishing the war and not removing Saddam Hussein from power during the desert storm war. Other people believe that the USA did not want to remove Saddam Hussein because he was a counterforce to Iran's radical regime. A weak Iraq would have boosted Iran's political and military dominance in the region.

This move on the other hand left a lot of unfinished business that could turn out to be costly at a later date. For instance, immediately after the war, the USA and the other desert storm allies encouraged the Kurds in the North and the Marsh Arabs in the south to start an uprising against Saddam Hussein. They were hoping that this would calumniate into a coup de' tat against Saddam Hussein. The two tribes are said to have been given confusing signals through radio, TV networks, and other channels that the U.S and its allies were behind them. The two tribes took up uprisings against the Saddam Hussein regime but they were brutally crushed by March 1991. Thousands and thousands of Kurds in the North escaped to the Kurdish areas in Turkey and Iran. It is believed that CIA operatives embedded with the Kurds in the north just vanished overnight and when the Saddam forces attacked the Kurds were left alone to face the music. This was a clear case of cut and run.

This way of handling issues reminded me of this American I met at a party in Mbarara Uganda. He was traveling through Uganda and I offered him accommodation together with his Ugandan girlfriend he had just met in Mbarara. One day after staying with me as a guest for one month or so he and the girl just vanished in thin air. I was worried stiff and started looking for them. I asked around for the girl's mother's place and after being directed, I rushed to find out if she had any information regarding these missing people. Fortunately, the mother told me that the girl had packed a suitcase and told her they would be back in a week's time.

After two months the girlfriend appeared and she told me that they had actually traveled to the neighboring country of Zaire. It appeared she had also been dumped and the man decided to move on with his mission. This goes to prove that communication is always vital and can save a lot of time and misunderstanding. The man could have just said goodbye to me or even left a note. To me, it was another unnecessary case of cut and run.

If the story of the CIA operatives deserting the Kurds in North Iraq is true, then I think it is unfortunate. It should have been wiser for them to tip off the Kurds or even ordered air support to buy the Kurds time to escape. A lot of lives would have been saved.

The USA and its allies could have in any case, finished off the job during the 100-hour ground attack instead of relying on a rebellion whose odds of winning was much worse than that of the mighty ducks. The desert storm allies had to mobilize half a million troops to uproot Hussein from Kuwait and there was no good reason to expect these tribes to uproot Saddam Hussein from power.

Due to these happenings and also because of the booming economy that had extended from the Reagan era which had started showing some signs of retraction, Bush's popularity soon evaporated and he lost the 1992 elections to Bill Clinton.

(F) The Clinton Era 1992-2000

Bill Clinton became president in 1992 and stayed in office until 2000. He was skillful enough to beat G.H.W. Bush whose popularity had been high in the '60s and '70s but had quickly evaporated. He became president when the cold war had just ended and was the first baby boomer to be president. He came to be known as the New Democrat because after failing to rule from the left, he shifted and ruled from the center and pulled off such policies as the North American Free Trade Agreement (NAFTA). The move to the center was necessary especially because the Republicans had gained majorities in Congress during the 1994 midterm elections.

During his presidency, Clinton enjoyed relative peace and became the first Democrat to win re-election since President Roosevelt. He enjoyed the extended prosperity from the Reagan era and became the first President in decades to produce a budget surplus. He was admired by many leaders, especially from the emerging democracies. They admired his style of governance because he is said to have treated them with respect and dignity. This is why so many African leaders wanted to emulate his style of diplomacy and governance. During his visit to Africa in 1998, there were so many loving crowds wanting to take a glimpse of this loving man. In Uganda, for instance, people were disappointed to see him flying instead of traveling by road so that they could shake hands. Africans like embracing and shaking hands but they could not realize that forces like international terrorists could not allow them to have a free hand in traveling by road while waving and shaking hands with the people.

In addition, Bill Clinton had the best shot at trying to achieve a comprehensive Middle East peace between Israel and the PLO. It is only Yasser Arafat, the PLO chairman who chickened out of the deal. Israel, under Yitzhak Rabin, was ready to accept the accords and give peace a chance to take root. It appears Arafat was under a lot of pressure from the extremists in his camp to not consent.

Despite having been impeached for the Monica Lewinski affair, Clinton left the presidency with the highest rating for a US president since WWII. Bill Clintons' ratings are still high today. President Clinton and G.H. Bush have since taken on so many humanitarian activities such as fundraising for the earthquake victims in the far east where over 200,000 people are believed to have perished. The two ex-presidents also undertook a similar mission for the victims of the Haiti earthquake where again so many people lost their lives. Bill Clinton remains the friend and a darling of very many people.

(G) GEORGE W. BUSH ERA 2000-2008

The GOP candidate George W. Bush was the elected president after the controversial year 2000 election against Al Gore of the Democratic Party. Since then and up to now, many democrats still accuse Bush of stealing the election. Some even said they would never recognize him as having been their president. Pro-left newspapers, TV network stations, and some people tried to ridicule and discredit the presidency of George Bush. Some of them continued giving the impression that he was wrong for America and wasn't smart enough to be their president. Many started mimicking the way he talked, walked, etc.

The good thing about G.W Bush is that he is focused so he ignored all these negative comments and concentrated on the big job he had just assumed. He had the big task of being the president of the USA. He knew what was expected of him as president and he went ahead and endeavored to govern to the best of his ability. That is why I think he is a man of true grit.

Trouble for Bush started well before he could fully start implementing his agenda of small government, reduced taxes, extended freedom, and security. On September 11, 2001, al Qaeda terrorists using highjacked planes attacked the USA mainland, bringing down the twin towers in New York, attacking the Pentagon headquarters in Washington DC, while the other plane that was destined to attack the White House was brought down by the courageous passengers in Pennsylvania. Over 3000 innocent people perished during these attacks. This act of terror against the U.S. would shape events and policies for the rest of Bush's presidency.

Immediately after the Al Qaeda attack, Bush and congress requested the Afghanistan government to handover Osama Bin Laden, so that he could stand trial for crimes committed against the USA and the free world at large. When the Afghanistan government refused to hand over Osama, Bush was left with no option but to declare war on Afghanistan, Al Qaeda, and world terrorism. Bush ordered the invasion of Afghanistan and the capture of Osama Bin Laden plus his supporters. Al Qaeda and other global terrorists in turn declared war against the USA and the free world. They made alliances with the Taliban to resist the US invasion of Afghanistan and its allies. They also vowed to attack the USA, its allies including their international interests anywhere in the world.

Since the bosses of Al-Qaeda had already boasted of having carried out the 911 attack and praised those attackers who carried out this cowardly act against innocent unarmed civilians, it was not a question of who did the attack but whether the US had the will and enough guts to bring these perpetrators to book.

The war in Afghanistan met with immediate success. The Afghanistan regime was overthrown and replaced with a more acceptable government. The overwhelming majority of Afghanistan's population supported the efforts of the coalition forces and the overthrow of the unpopular and oppressive regime.

The Afghanistan people started enjoying the feeling of freedom and human rights. Women and children who were liberated are now enjoying exercising the freedom and liberty which had been denied to them for so long. Previously Afghanistan women had no power to express their views and were mandated to cover themselves almost the whole body including their faces leaving a small tear to see through with their eyes. Girls were not considered important enough to attend school. Now, all children of both sexes have started attending real schools of knowledge and not just for religious studies.

The NATO forces nearly captured Osama Bin Laden but he escaped to the more mountainous and rugged areas between Afghanistan and Pakistan. It is the hope of many that one day he will be captured and brought to answer for his activities against the US and especially the over 3000 innocent people who were killed by his attackers on September 11, 2001. It is however gratifying and important to note that many of Osama's lieutenants and many of his supporters have either been killed or captured. Osama Bin Laden and more of his lieutenants have since been killed during the Obama administration.

The coalition efforts in Afghanistan seemed to be paying off and were now producing positive results. Therefore since George W Bush had breathing space, in 2003 he decided to also turn his attention to other international pending issues. He immediately turned his attention to deal with the problems in Iraq. He gave an ultimatum to Saddam Hussein who had defiled so many of the United Nations' resolutions, to either abide by the resolution or face the consequences. Iraq had failed to account for their stockpiles of weapons of mass destruction which they had claimed to possess. Saddam Hussein ignored all these warnings and continued to ridicule the UN and he even had the audacity of expelling the UN observers who had been posted to Iraq. Saddam Hussein continued also to ridicule and confront many other leaders whenever it suited him. Bush urged him at least leave quietly but he would still not comply because he still thought the UN was a paper tiger.

The UN could not take it any longer and with the backing of the USA and other western powers, they authorized the use of force against Iraq. Since Iraq still refused to listen even to the last-minute ultimatum, George Bush, who was not prepared to see this behavior continue, ordered the invasion of Iraq in 2003 with over 30 other nations participating.

After about 2 months of Arial bombing, the ground war commenced and the Iraq Government was overthrown soon after and a broad-based regime was put in place. Bush though made a tactical and political error when he declared that the mission had been accomplished. The war was designed to be a short-lived operation and for a while, everything seemed to be going as planned. The USA government had calculated that the Iraqis would take over the running of the new government and assume the security responsibilities of replacing the UN forces in Iraq. It appears the Iraqi anti-Hussein people had given the impression that Saddam Hussein would be replaced by a popular regime.

Here in the US, the population was behind GW Bush and in 2004 he was re-elected. On top of that, the Republicans increased their majority in Congress.

After a while, however, the success of US forces and its allies in Iraq started faltering. There was too much infighting among the different Iraq factions. The Sunnis could not agree with the Shiites. The Kurds in the north also had their own demands.

The Saddam Hussein forces that had been disgraced and dismissed started regrouping and had now started fighting back. The Saddam Hussein civil servants who had been laid off also joined the rebellion. Al Qaeda and other terror groups saw this as an opportunity to fight and defeat the USA and its coalition forces in Iraq. Al Qaeda, therefore, built up alliances with the Sunni population, and the remnants of the defeated and disgraced Saddam military, police, and other security forces. Other foreign volunteer terror forces also joined in this crusade. It was technically not wise for the new Iraq government to have dismissed all the Saddam military personnel. The combined forces waged a counteroffensive and slowly but surely put the US and its coalition forces on the defensive. Countries like Iran, N. Korea, Syria, and Lebanon gave open support to Al Qaeda, their allies, and the local disgruntled groups. It is alleged that they even supplied them with logistical support. The USA and coalition causalities were mounting especially from the roadside bombs. This turn of events affected Bush's popularity. He watched his popularity rating drop from the '70s to below 50 percent.

Indeed in the 2006 midterm elections, Bush and Republicans lost control of Congress. This turn of events did not help Bush and the Republicans as news of casualties was broadcast and discussed whenever any American soldiers were killed or wounded. There were barrages of constant negative sentiments made by left-wing newspapers, TV network stations, and many of the political leaders from the Democratic Party stating that the USA was losing the Iraq war. Then there was the move by Cindy Sheehan who went to Bush's home in Texas to protest against the Iraq war.

However, GW Bush was not intimidated as he focused on winning the war against terror in Iraq and elsewhere. He ordered, against all odds, for more troops to be sent to Iraq when the majority of the population, Democratic Party members in the Congress, and even some Republicans were urging Bush to abandon the war and withdraw from Iraq. President Bush went ahead and appointed General Petraeus to lead the American forces and allies in a counteroffensive against Al Qaeda and its supporters. General Petraeus reorganized the coalition forces. He partnered with the rest of the Iraq population and after many fierce encounters, the terrorist forces started weakening. The terrorist forces suffered casualties and then seemed to have melted in thin air.

General Petraeus had achieved what many people thought was impossible to accomplish. When General Petraeus came to report to Congress about what was going on in Iraq, some politicians were so frustrated and started calling him General Betrayus instead of Petraeus. Maybe because they did not like his success in Iraq which could have restored Bush's credibility and revive the popularity of the Republicans.

Bush is not a quitter and America came out victorious with dignity. Although the ground war had been won, the political solutions in Iraq are still elusive and answers still must be found.

Apart from the Iraq war, the Bush administration was also confronted with many other issues. There was the Katrina catastrophe on August 28th, 2005. Bush admitted that the disaster was not well handled. A great percentage of the 60 billion dollars allocated to solve the problems created by the disaster was either misallocated or misspent. Billions of dollars were wasted and much of it was not properly accounted for. This has left many residents of New Orleans and Mississippi who were affected by Katrina still suffering till today. Katrina showed how a country with so much expertise and strict accounting procedures can fail to deal with what appeared to be a straightforward issue. The people of New Orleans and Mississippi were almost reduced to third-world status. One frustrated lady asked why all the bad things should happen when Bush was in power, citing September 11 among other problems.

Indeed in 2007 came the housing bubble and economic meltdown. What was amazing and surprising was that before the causes of the disaster were analyzed, people were already blaming Bush as the guilty party. He had to be the one responsible and take the blame. Indeed it is said that up to now, nobody appears to have taken time, trouble, or much bother to find the real causes of the global economic and housing chaos other than just putting the blame on Bush. That is why the problems have not been fully resolved up to today. It appears they are trying all sorts of haphazard solutions. It is like treating malaria with antibiotics as they continue with these trial and error solutions.

Some people blame the Iraq war expenses as the root cause of these problems. Other people, however, believe that the $900 billion spent by the Bush administration on the war effort in Iraq and Afghanistan, is not the main underlining cause that led to these economic problems. They pointed out that among others the faulty housing policies which allowed people to take on big and expensive homes they could not sustain or service on a long-term basis could have been one of the main underlying causes. Furthermore, they believe that many of these overvalued mortgage loans and notes were unfortunately sold to Fannie Mae and Freddie Mac which were created by Congress. Fannie Mae and Freddie Mac are now holding these overvalued mortgage papers which could be in the trillions. Many other local and foreign banks and institutions are also holding the same types of overvalued papers. This is why many people think the housing problem not only affected the US but also many other countries and hence it became a global problem that needed a global solution.

Other people believe that faulty economic policies were also responsible for the economic meltdown. They believe that lack of leveled ground had encouraged many corporations to take dangerous and poor business investments which made them vulnerable when bad days come to confront them. America was no longer competitive as it had priced itself out of the world market business. The economic meltdown, therefore, caught them with their pants down.

Signs were there showing the impending disaster but nobody including Congress took any corrective measures such as recapitalization policies to counter the hard times.

There was corporate greed and the only thing which mattered was to declare record profits, some of which were false. Disasters such as the Enron Scandal should have been a clear warning sign.

When it came to what to do to address the economic and housing problems, it is the opinion of many people that Bush errored by using taxpayers' money to keep these faltering companies and institutions afloat by reasoning that they were too big to fail. Furthermore, the exercise was also unfortunately done in a selective manner as if small-scale businesses and people did not deserve attention. His administration infused a lot of the taxpayers' money into companies and institutions without even seeking their shareholders' approval. There was no clear arrangement under which the money was disbursed. Companies that could not possibly survive should have been left to go under because they were being run by undisciplined managers. It is alleged that some CEOs of these undisciplined companies have insured themselves by setting up connections within the public service. Some of them get government business usually on a favorable, unfair non-competitive selective basis where the spirit of fair competition is usually not applied. Others get special treatment by getting interest-free taxpayers' money as they did when the economy and housing business collapsed in 2007. All in all, they are parasitic on the taxpayers in every imaginable way. Some of these companies have set up all sorts of exemptions from Congress so that they hardly pay any corporation tax and therefore in every way they are always winners. On the other side, it is also alleged that these CEO also holds a grip on their company's boards mainly because they have a hand in the appointment of company board members. Many of the board members of these companies owe their allegiance to these CEOs and other executives instead of the shareholders who are supposed to have appointed them. The CEOs use these advantages to influence bad policies for their institutions. Many of these CEOs have worked out favorable terms of service which gives them salaries and handshakes. Some of them have made provisions in their terms of service which allows them to be paid bonuses even when the companies make losses or even when the companies go bankrupt. A bonus is supposed to be paid to someone who has made exceptional profits.

These executives, therefore, tend to control the shareholders and public servants because of the above-advanced reasons to make sure that either way they are winners. When the going is bad, they fall on their buddies in the public service who bail them out with the taxpayers' money to keep their companies afloat. Because they have a grip on the boards there is a tendency for board members to side with the company executives, whenever there is a problem with the shareholders.

To make matters worse now government went further and grabbed many of these companies and they are now government-owned.

The risk is now on the taxpayer and not those reckless CEOS' and their executive officers. It is a pity that government does not respect company law and has illegally grabbed and taken over the running of these once-private companies such as GM and AIG. The government has illegally taken over the shareholders' interests in these companies. This is a blow to the concept of free-market capitalism and private ownership. It is now risky to invest without the fear of interference from the government. People can no longer feel safe owning their own assets without fear of being grabbed by the government in the name of too big to fail. The principle of private ownership and bankruptcy procedures must be restored if innovation and private business risk-taking are not going to be compromised. Let the people who invest in business take the risk of suffering losses or making profits. If the government does not unnecessarily keep these dying companies afloat, new and disciplined enterprises will always emerge. That is the way the capitalist free market system is supposed to operate. It is a system of competition to produce results the most efficient way. A partial or complete takeover of private companies in the name of public interest or concern is usually a policy found in socialist or communist economies. It appears the USA is following and set to looking more like some of the socialist countries in Europe. USA solutions differ from European solutions although they are allies. The USA must decide whether it is leading the economy in a socialist way rather than taking piecemeal action in that direction.

George. W. Bush made some other policies that were appreciated. For instance, he spearheaded the $15 billion HIV Aids global initiatives which helped many African and other emerging democracies to tackle this dangerous and almost impossible disease whose characteristics have made it difficult to find a cure. When Bush took the African tour, he was greeted like a true hero. The ordinary people were so grateful for the Aid which helped so many communities to combat the Aids disease and as a result, so many lives were saved.

Here at home Bush also tried to solve the problems of Social Security and Immigration. Although unsuccessful, at least he attempted to address and find solutions to these long outstanding problems. As regards the social security problem, Bush looked at so many options and suggestions, such as the possibility of raising the retirement age by up to 5 years because people are now living longer. Bush also zeroed on privatizing the fund by allowing the subscribers to open up private personal accounts to be managed by the account holders. The measures did not take off because many representatives from congress from the two parties lacked the will to tackle these sensitive issues. These measures were unlikely to pass since the Democrats controlled Congress. The idea of private social security, private accounts should not be discouraged even if it was not considered. It can be part of a basket of investment options for the fund. It is important to adopt smart ideas which maximize returns for the fund holders.

In this regard, I have my experiences in another but similar social security program. This happened in Uganda when the government set up a social security fund program in 1965. The employer and employee each contributed 5 percent towards the fund. I was working with Grindlays bank at the time and by the time I left bank employment I had saved up to the equivalent of US $ 10,000 in the fund. Since I was recently entitled to draw on the fund I sent an inquiry to find out the value of my account in the fund. To my surprise, I came to find out that the value of my account in the fund was only Uganda shilling 20,000, and the dollar equivalent at Uganda Shillings 2200 per US dollar, amounted to less than the US $ 10. Imagine investing the US $ 10,000 and ending up with the US $ 10. If I had been given a chance to have a hand in investing my money, I would have made better choices such as putting the money in US$ related portfolios so that I am not caught by hyperinflation which is prevailing in so many emerging economies. When I invested in the fund the currency exchange rate was 7.5 Uganda shillings to the dollar. However, now the rate has settled at about 2200 Ugandan Shillings to the dollar as a result of various bad policies of the previous regimes. The value of my investment is now almost negligible. I could also have invested my money in assets such as property or even bought cows because they multiply, in numbers and value.

I, therefore, concur with Bush and other people who believe that investors should have a say in how their money is invested. Returns must be higher than inflation in order to make economic sense in the first place.

As far as Immigration is concerned G. W. Bush tried but was failed by congress. Reasons for this failure will also be mentioned later in the book while discussing immigration issues. What is important is that this matter should be approached on a non-bipartisan basis. Indeed this bill had bipartisan support in the senate and this time there was an effort from both sides to find a comprehensive solution to the immigration problem. The effort failed because there was a negative reaction from some republican Senators who called it amnesty and Democrats in the House who made it impossible for a compromise to pass at the committee stage. Another great opportunity to tackle the problem was missed. This was sad because the majority of the population wanted their legislators to take courage and find a comprehensive solution to the Immigration problem.

When Bush did something he believed in it and did everything he could to make it succeed. I hope history will judge him much more favorably than he has been portrayed by so many, especially those who wanted to make political capital out of it for one reason or another.

(H) BARACK OBAMA 2009 TO DATE

It is not easy to make the same comparisons for President Barack Obama because he has only been in office for hardly two years. He is yet to finish his four-year term in office. I will however make some statements on what remarks and observations many people have made.

Many observers especially from the Conservative camp believe that he has not yet fully adjusted himself from being the candidate to being the President. It is important to realize that once President, you lead all those who voted for you and those who did not vote for you. The need for moderating the tone of language when one is the president of all the people is of paramount importance. The Republicans are claiming that he is still blaming Bush and his administration for anything bad happening but credits himself for any positive good news. This is the usual temptation for many presidents as they continue blaming the other side once they assume office because they don't want to associate themselves with failure. The Republicans and Independents are blaming him for not practicing the new politics he promised America of being the uniter rather than the divider of the population. Others also say that since he told the American people that he had solutions to America's economic and other problems left by the Bush Administration, it is important for him to forget Bush and move on implementing what he promised the country.

At the beginning of his presidency, President Obama got Congress to approve almost what he wanted. After all, he had majorities in both houses of Congress. He asked for the Recovery Stimulus money and congress passed the bill without much scrutiny. If the Stimulus Act does not produce the promised results then he should have no one else to blame. The American people will listen and understand the reasons when the anticipated results are delayed or not being realized. If however, you do not tell them the truth, they will punish you during the next elections.

President Obama's second major legislative business was the Health Care and Education Reform Act of 2010 which amended the Patient Protection and Affordable Care Act of 2010. This 2400 page act was also passed in Congress without much scrutiny, debate, or assessment on its social and financial impact on the economy. Members of the House of Representatives were told to first vote for the bill and read the details later. In the Senate, when the Republican members wanted to raise amendments they were generally denied that chance. When it appeared that the bill would not pass through the senate, the speaker used the nuclear option to have the bill passed by a simple majority.

As a result, it is no wonder the act is facing a lot of challenges from many quarters. These include lawsuits from some of the States, Republicans, many other institutions, individuals, and on top of all this, the majority of the population is still opposed to the act. The republicans ceased on this opportunity to discredit the bill and indeed during the 2010 midterm elections the republicans promised that they were going to repeal the act. The Republicans used the act as one of the main campaign issues. This tactic paid off because the Republicans gained a net of sixty-three members in the House of Representatives. They also nearly regained control of the Senate.

The other major bill which the president introduced through Congress was the Energy bill. Although the bill was passed by the House of Representatives with little debate, it was blocked in the Senate. The main criticism of the bill was that it was going to increase energy costs for ordinary households. The bill also had over 1,000 pages and not too easily understood by many people.

After the Democrats were rebuffed in November 2010 midterm elections, the President surprised many people by changing his tone and he started promising to negotiate with Republicans so that the country can move forward. During the January 2011 annual state of the union nation address, the president appeared to be shifting to the center in his approach. He was even challenging republicans to come up with ideas and work with him. He promised to seek compromise with congress to find pro-American solutions and move the country forward. The president even indicated that he would be willing to amend parts of the Health Care act by removing some of the bad and contentious provisions. He also promised to embrace good republican ideas regarding healthcare. These two moves have since boosted the president's rating and now he appears to be a formidable and almost unbeatable candidate for the 2012 presidential elections. This has left the Republicans with the big task of finding a candidate who can beat President Obama in 2012. That candidate must be able to approach issues from the center and not from the extreme right.

President Obama is however still stuck with many left-leaning Tsars, whom he appointed since he became president. To many people, it appears that these Tsars have caused conflict within the administration, especially as regards policy positions on many issues. There appear to be differences in approach between the Tsars and the appointed Secretaries. It appears that some of the Tsars have become more authoritative over certain issues than the Secretaries. Secretaries are supposed to advise initiate and implement policies as assigned to them by the President. As it may appear that some of the Tsars have taken some of this role and therefore the power and role of the Secretaries may have been compromised to some extent. There are unconfirmed reports that some of the Secretaries have not had an audience with their boss since taking office. Some people hold the opinion that it may be easier for some of the Tsars to interact with the president. Future events will therefore determine the presidency of President Barack Obama.

CONCLUDING REMARKS

EXECUTIVE POWERS AND
CONCLUDING REMARKS

The above reviews of the recent Presidents show the growing power of the Executive Branch and mainly at the expense of Congress. Congress seems to be contented with this state of affairs as they powerlessly watch their powers and influence diminish as time passes by. The unpopularity of Congress which now stands at less than 20%, which is far below that of the Executive has made matters worse. In the next chapter, we shall examine and point out the main problems of Congress and also suggest ways of how Congress can address these issues and slowly regain its role and responsibilities as originally envisaged in the constitution

CHAPTER 5

CONGRESS

A1) HISTORY AND TRANSFORMATION

It is important to note that Congress has undergone a lot of changes over the years. Indeed from around 1775, congressional powers expanded over the years and the following years are important landmarks. They highlight the way these powers and responsibilities have evolved over the mentioned years. These significant reform years are 1776, 1781, 1787, 1910, and 1913. There were also reforms in the 1970s and 1990's which improved and strengthened the functions of the committees in both houses.

As already indicated, the Constitution vests all legislative powers in the bicameral congress. The Constitution also empowers Congress to impose taxes, levies and to oversee the implementation of these funds. Additional functions include commerce, finance, budgeting, and appropriation of funds.

Other extra functions and responsibilities are enumerated in Article 1 Section 8 of the constitution. Congress was designed to be a very strong institution with almost unlimited powers.

(A2) INFLUENCE:

In the course of exercising its functions, the level of congressional influence over the executive has varied from time to time mainly depending on the leadership in congress. It also depends on congressional boldness to diminish the political influence of the presidency in pushing its programs in congress. Usually, the presidency has more cloud if the leadership in congress belongs to their party and or if the leadership in Congress is not very influential. However, it is important to note that over the years the presidency has generally assumed more and more legislative and budgetary powers at the expense of congress.

A3) CONGRESSIONAL OVERSIGHT:

In addition, congressional oversight over the executive and judiciary has also lapsed over the years. This is a constitutional responsibility but Congress is treating this responsibility less seriously than it should be. The other two branches seem to be happy getting away with many instances of acting outside the purpose for which congress passes bills and appropriated funds thereof. The two branches have noticed that Congress is less and less active in querying how laws are being implemented and how appropriated funds are being spent. Recent examples of these instances include illegal wiretapping of citizens' telephones during the G.W. Bush administration. Then there is also the spending of the stimulus funds by both Bush and Obama administrations outside the purposes for which Congress had approved the funds. This lack of oversight seriously undermines the effectiveness of congress in seeing that the laws and funds as passed by congress are being respected and implemented accordingly. This in the long-run has gradually diminished the power, effectiveness, and respect of congress.

A4) OTHER FACTORS AFFECTING CONGRESS:

Congress is also being influenced and affected in performance of its functions in the following ways:

A4.1) POLITICAL ACTION COMMITTEES:

Political action committees affect the way congress votes. These committees have grown from 600 to over 3800 and their annual campaign contributions to legislators have grown from approximately $10 million to over $120 million. This is a lot of money and affects the way congress votes or delays action on issues.A4.2) Other special interests, in addition, there are also lobbyists and other special interest groups who also influence the way congress performs. It is said that sometimes these committees and pressure groups often draft bills for Congress to consider. For instance, it is alleged that groups such as the Apollo Alliance wrote the stimulus bill. These special interest groups have grown to over 4500, which include the different business interests, labor unions,s, etc. It is therefore becoming increasingly more and more difficult for the political representatives in Congress to either vote with their conscience or following the positions of their constituents. The constituents' interests and opinions seem to have been diminishing over the years and it appears they no longer take first priority. Many of the voters' demands are either dropped from being debated or if they are debated no final decision is ever taken, on these important matters.

(A) PARTY INFLUENCES:
A5.1) PARTY SET UP:

The Party setup and mechanism also affect the way Congress functions. The U.S. has a multiparty system but only two parties have dominated American politics. We have the Conservative Republican Party (GOP) and the more liberal Democratic Party. There are many other small parties such as the Green party, The Libertarian Party, Independence Party, the Reform Party, and Constitution party, etc. Individuals can also stand for political office as independents. There are currently two independents in the Senate although they are associated and caucus with the Democratic Party. The two main political parties are almost equal in strength and since Congress seems to vote along party lines, the business in Congress has recently become polarized and very little business appears to have a chance of passing. The people's business has stalled and people have lost faith in Congress as the political organ which can find solutions to their problems. The rating of congress which had fallen to 20% has deteriorated even further since the November 2010 mid-term elections. The interests of the American people are no longer the prime concern of Congress.

A5.2) LACK OF DEFINED PARTY ACTION PLANS:

The parties do not have a defined long-term plan of action of what they will do to solve the critical problems facing the nation. The parties are more interested in negative politics against one another and looking for anything that can enable them to win the next elections. The parties have flip-flopped over issues such as the economy, immigration, health care, social security only to mention but a few and they keep moving in directions where the wind is blowing. They support whatever is likely to bring them back in power during the next elections. It is no longer based on principles such as free-market concepts. For instance, during the 2008 elections, the Democratic Party won because they promised to change. They promised that the change would give solutions and lead to quick economic and housing recovery. There was however no detailed definitions of these plans or explanations on how this change would solve these problems. Few voters questioned or asked for any details on how this change would create jobs and lead to economic recovery since this was their primary concern. They were more interested in ending the 8 years of the Bush dynasty and were ready to vote for anything that was opposing Bush. Anybody who dared to question about details of the promise of hope was considered to be against the change wave. The independent voters who are normally the swing voters this time also overwhelmingly voted for change. There were no short or long-term plans in the change program, just change to wherever you want to take me.

Two years later during the November 2010 mid-term elections the tables had tumbled and turned. The people were now disappointed that the undefined promised change had not fully produced the expected results. Unemployment had risen to 9.2% instead of going down to 8% as projected. The massive 2400 page health care act was already having problems mainly because it is not what the majority of the people really wanted.

The Republican Party, therefore, had seized this chance to punch holes both in the health care act and the economic recovery program. During the November 2010 mid-term elections the Democrats lost control of the House of Representatives with a net loss of 63 seats. The Democrats barely managed to hang on to the Senate. The swing independent voters this time voted Republican and hoped that maybe this time the Republicans will deliver. However once again it appears they are being tossed from frying pan to fire. They are once again waiting for answers to their problems. They want jobs, jobs, and solutions to the economy. The Republicans did not win because they had solutions to the problems of the electorate. They only won because the Democrats did not fully deliver.

After the mid-term elections what was surprising is that the first thing that Republicans did was to take on the issue of earmarks instead of dealing with the real people's problems such as jobs, budget shortfalls, the ever ballooning national debt, and how to solve the housing meltdown problems. This is mainly because they do not have a program of action to address these issues which can lead to the recovery of the economy. The earmarks were not the peoples' main campaign issue as it accounted for a small percentage of what could be done to reduce the excessive government expenditure and national debt. No wonder the rating of Congress has dropped to 13% even after the November 2010 mid-term elections.

After the GOP made gains in Congress, the public was eagerly waiting to hear action from them regarding jobs, jobs, and jobs and on how to improve the economy, also the budget deficits and the looming national debt. The GOP had promised during the 2010 midterm election campaigns to reduce government spending and improve or repeal the Health Care Act. These were some of the main Republican campaign promises and they were expected to deliver. They had a challenge because at that time there was a pending 1.2 trillion spending bill. The people would have been more pleased to know that Republicans in Congress were rejecting the spending bill because they were not given enough time to read, understand and debate the details of the bill. Instead, they and the right-wing media were 24/7 busy debating the banning earmarks. The earmarks issue was not the number one campaign issue. That's why the public has a very low opinion of congress because of the window dressing approach to their problems. Congress should have instead moved and cleaned up the 1.2 million dollar expenditure bill. They would have taken time plucking out items especially those smuggled in by lobbyists, political groups, and other pressure groups, That is where the main spending problem lies. In many other countries, the legislature discusses and pronounces itself on every clause of the bill. In this way, even the legislators who did not have the opportunity or time to study the bill have a chance of giving their inputs when they spot some glaringly bad clauses in the bill, instead of spending days discussing earmarks which are less than 5% of the total expenditure.

Both two parties are not in a mood to address the real main issues at hand. They seem to be satisfied with the status quo. This reminds me of a friend who always loved to take life easy. He would always sing the song that life was Ob-La-Di, Ob-la-Da and life goes on. It is nice to hear when politicians say that doing nothing is not an option but in reality, they appear to be doing nothing regarding the real issues. Congress must endeavor to take people's business very seriously because the destiny for so many people depends on Congress taking correct decisions on their behalf. This is their duty as they were elected just to do that. Congress must find a way to deliver in one way or the other.

Unfortunately, Congress is once again polarized. Congress must find a formula and begin to work for America and not just for the sake of working of winning general elections and paying back various special interest groups who funded their elections.

(A6) NEED FOR STRUCTURAL CHANGES OF CONGRESS:

Congress as is needed to be examined and see whether some changes can make it function more effectively. The following items some of the ideas which could be debated and considered.

(A6.I) AMEND TWO YEAR TERM OF THE HOUSE OF REPRESENTATIVES:

This is a problem which Congress and the public should address. There is a need to improve on or reform the two-year tenure of the House of Representatives. There is a strong opinion by many people; that the two-year tenure is too short for the representatives to effectively serve the people. The presidency has a four-year term which gives the office holder at least two to three years to serve the people without worrying too much about getting ready for the next general elections. The Senate has a tenure of 6 years which gives the Senators at least 4 years to serve the people without election worries. With the house of representatives, the members have hardly one year before they start thinking about the next elections. This hardly gives them enough time to deal with the peoples' business before they are troubled with election worries. This phenomenon affects the way house representatives' vote on peoples' issues. This is because they hardly have enough time to settle since the next election is around the corner.

One Representative who was being interviewed on television said that soon after representatives take office they are immediately bombarded with all sorts of demands from different groups. They are most of all reminded that the next elections are not too far and therefore they must start getting ready. They are told by the party leaders how the Representative should vote on certain matters although the Representative might not have been part of the decision making for that part of party policy. They also get communication from the Executive on how he should vote on certain issues or risk delay in implementing projects in their areas or even worse. Their constituents start demanding and telling them how they should vote on certain matters. They also demand as to what projects they should be pushed in their areas. The Representatives now remember that they can no longer load pork on any bill to solve some of the constituents burning issues because of the decision they took recently. They now realize that they can't even use this constitutional right to serve their constituents. Then they are reminded by special interest groups of how they should vote if they hope to receive any campaign financing. Even the news media is on their necks threatening to expose any representative who might intend to vote differently from certain party positions on any particular issue. It is now politics of fear. All these developments do not give the representatives enough time to settle in their offices and legislate effectively for their areas and the country. This most likely affects the way most representative votes in the house.

This is a good cause why the house of representative tenure to be increased from two to four years. A 4-year term will help the representatives to settle down and tackle the unsolved hot issues such as social security, health care, immigration, economic growth, jobs, etc more effectively. The House Representatives need breathing space of two years during which they can legislate effectively without too many pressures on them. They will end up producing better legislative results for their constituents and the country at large.

(A6.II) EARMARKS:

The issue of whether Congress should limit and reduce its constitutional legislative powers by abolishing pork took center stage when Congress resumed session immediately after the 2010 midterm elections. The constitution was originally designed to give Congress almost unlimited legislative powers. The new conservatives especially in the House of Representatives spearheaded abolishing the use of pork during the new congressional legislative debates. Even the last stand in the Senate had to give in because all of a sudden the new Congress appeared to blame that pork was the main reason responsible for budget deficits and the national debt.

Even the President who had originally used pork to effectively serve his area said that since Congress wants to reduce their legislative powers and make the presidency more powerful would be with that. He therefore quickly said that if Congress brings any bill containing pork, He would use the veto power and reject the bill. I understand that instead of the term pork they now call them extras. Pork, if exercised properly, helps Members of Congress to fill in gaps that might have been overlooked by the executive while budgeting. By refusing to exercise this power is another sign of the weakening powers of Congress at their own expense. This time it is Congress shooting itself in the foot. Congress should stop the culture of overreacting whenever there is a perceived problem. If there was a problem with how to deal with earmarks, Congress should instead have set up a procedure of dealing with earmarks and continue to serve the constituents of forgotten areas who do not have lobbyists to fight for them. There are members of Congress who do not belong to the high circles of power and do not yet have enough influence. So the only weapon they have to bring service nearer to their people is to use the legislative power of pork. All Congress needs to do is to control excessive use of pork through the introduction of procedures and guidelines. The culture of overreacting by the Executive and Congress does not always produce the right results. For instance, there was an oil spill and drilling was suspended, it is like suspending driving on the roads because of a car accident. When there was the mistreatment of prisoners in Guantanamo they wanted to close the facility instead of changing the rules at the prison. This culture of overreacting for populist reasons as a way of a quick fix for solving problems can sometimes lead to making irrational and bad decisions.

It is important for Congress to debate issues in a calm manner and look for appropriate solutions. This is what the Constitution and the people want and expect them to do.

It appears that Congress has put itself in a position that has enabled the other two branches to expand at their expense. Congress must therefore take urgent steps to regain public trust and improve on its ratings which have sunk further down to 13% since the 2010 mid-term elections.

Congress must make the necessary sacrifices and make changes as to the way it conducts its business so that it can better serve the people. Non-performance and abdication of the constitutional responsibility by Congress should become a thing of the past. It has also been observed that Congress has been sitting fewer and fewer days as the years pass by.

(7) IDEAS AND ACTIONS FOR IMPROVING CONGRESS:

Below are some of the ideas that congress should address.

(I) SITTING DAYS:

There are suggestions that congress has been meeting less and fewer days allocated to conduct the people's business. This is not good when there are so many pending unsolved important issues. Congress must therefore revisit this issue and make the necessary adjustments.

(2) ELECTORAL PROCESS:

The electoral process needs Congressional attention in the following areas:

(I) VOTING MACHINES

Congress should resolve the voting machines' complaints. There have been many issues regarding the voting machines. These machines are said to be vulnerable to various types of malpractices. The possibilities include the following:

- a. They can be commanded or programmed to reject some or particular candidate votes.
- b. They can allow stuffing of votes.
- c. Some can be manipulated to start with a high figure other than Zero.

d. Others could be manipulated to give false results.

e. No one can forget the 2000 problem of dimples because the machines could not properly pierce some of the ballot papers and this made it difficult to clearly show the voter's intent.

f. Some of the machines were so complicated that, especially minority voters, found them difficult to understand in those few minutes one takes to vote and as a result, many minorities have a higher percentage of spoilt votes. This can therefore disenfranchise many people.

g. Many of the machines experience mechanical failures. If there is a mechanical failure of some sort many of the machines do not have backup systems. There are complaints that companies and people with technology which they claimed could eliminate most of these voting machines complaints have been sidelined and even denied to demonstrate their alternate systems. This is mainly because of the vested interests who have used their contacts and influence to block any competition both at the Federal and State levels. If this is true it is absurd because any move which blocks democratic practices must be fought and eliminated at all costs. I do not have concrete facts but Congress and States can easily investigate these claims and take corrective measures. I have, however, seen a documentary which seems to talk about the complaints of these aggrieved companies or parties.

Solutions For Voting Machines

(a) The federal and state electoral boards should sit and share views and recommend the best systems and standards which must be adhered to by all parties.

(b) Aggrieved companies should be allowed to demonstrate what they have. Backup systems in case of machine failure or sabotage should and must be part of the solution.

(II) Vote Rigging.

The States and Congress must listen to any complaints of vote-rigging and misreporting and take corrective measures in order to avoid and discourage such unfortunate and undemocratic practices

(III) Voter Rights Awareness.

Teaching materials and lessons. The Electoral systems both at the federal and state level should arrange for civil lessons regarding all sorts of issues about their election rights, laws and regulations well before election time. They should also synthesize the population especially minorities as regards the voting machine systems.

(IV) Ex-Convicts Voting Rights:

Both the federal and state legislators should look at the complaints by ex-convicts of being disenfranchised. There have been complaints that there are too many restrictions by various states which make it difficult for ex-convicts to exercise their rights to vote as allowed by the Constitution. For instance, in Florida. ex-convicts are denied the right to vote until they pay-off their court fines.

In the free democratic system, it is important for Congress to deal expeditiously with issues regarding the electoral process. If people lose confidence in the electoral system, the whole democratic process is likely to be jeopardized.

CHAPTER 6

VI) REFORM OF THE PARTY PRIMARIES

As mentioned before, politics in the USA is based on party politics. It is important to keep the system as democratic as possible. Further reforms which Congress and the States should make include the following points; USA should be seen as a democratic country respected and admired by the general public and everyone else. This process begins with the way the party mechanism works to elect its political leaders. This begins with the election of political party representatives for various offices through the holding of elections. In the USA this process begins by selecting political party candidates through a process known as primaries. The voting system used in holding these party primaries should in principle reflect the will of the people. This could be best done by adopting a simple democratic uniform voting system. However, currently different parties, states use various voting systems and regulations while holding their political party primaries.

For instance, during the 2008 Presidential elections, both the Republican and Democratic parties held presidential primaries. For the Republicans, this was so because President Bush had completed his two terms of office. However, the main struggle and interest were within the Democratic Party primaries between the candidates who had been in waiting for eight years for a chance to become the next president and unseat the Republican Party for the post, and indeed the primaries produced a lot of fireworks.

The process in both parties was very competitive. Congressional primaries were also taking place at the same time but the main focus was on the presidential primaries and this is where we shall focus our main comments regarding the system, problems, and possible suggestions for holding primaries to select political party candidates who will represent the party on the voting day.

(A) The Voting system

First of all, the voting system in the Democratic Party primaries is not uniform. There is no clear simple voting system as we see in the many elections where the winner takes all. Some states allow only party members to vote, while others allow other groups such as the Independents, and even others allow every qualified voter to participate. Other states use the caucusing voting system. This system does not appear to be very democratic as it does not encourage the universal concept of one man one vote. However, the caucus system helps the unknowns to introduce themselves to the general public through public meetings and door-to-door retail politics.

In Uganda for instance, after the 1986 takeover of government by a popular revolution, we had a movement system where everybody belonged to the movement. Candidates vying for political office were not allowed to hold rallies but could hold caucus meetings attended by all the candidates at times and venues agreed upon by the candidates. Each candidate speaks to the audience for 10 minutes or as agreed to say why he/she is the best person to represent them. The audience then asks questions during the question time. Candidates were also allowed to the campaign by going from house to house. In the end, on the polling day, all registered voters cast their votes for their favorite candidate. The system helps candidates with little money to participate and sometimes they win. The system has since been replaced by the conventional multi-party primaries voting system but all the primaries elections for party candidates take place on the same day. There are now at least 6 registered parties in the country in a multi-party presidential type system.

The other main drawback for the caucus system is that it does not allow the secrecy of the person to vote the way they truly feel at heart.

(B) Voting schedules

Another rule is that states the DNC allocates dates when the various states should hold their primaries. States such as Florida and Michigan have been complaining that under the present system they hardly participate in choosing their party representative for the presidential and other elections. By the time the voting comes to Florida and Michigan, the Democratic Party candidate is most likely already known. States such as Iowa and New Hampshire where the primaries always commence get undue influence in determining who would be the Presidential candidate for either of the two parties. This time Florida and Michigan decided to vote early and for trying to do so and therefore participate in the nominating process of their party candidates, they were punished by both Republican and Democratic Parties by striping the size of their delegations by 50%. This problem is definitely undemocratic and both parties need to urgently address this problem and look for a way that is more democratic, fair, and inclusive for all the states. The Republican Party's innovation which allows states to vote early but candidates share delegates based on a percentage basis, seems to be a good solution. States which allow winner takes all can then vote after super Tuesday. This is good because it is unlikely for any candidate to have amassed enough votes to win by Super Tuesday. The other States will therefore still remain relevant in the primary elections and decisions.

(C) Allocation of delegates

The other issue in the Democratic Party machinery is that delegates are allocated according to what percentage they obtain in the primaries. This is getting more and more difficult for one candidate to obtain the necessary votes to win the primary elections by the end of the exercise. In the Democratic Party where super delegates make up about 20% of the total delegates at the DNC meeting, their influence becomes pronounced if no candidate has secured enough delegates to claim the nomination. These super delegates could end up deciding the party's candidate thus making the process not so democratic. The process, therefore, needs to be reviewed and improved upon.

(D) SUPER DELEGATES

The super delegates are made up of members of congress, senior members of the DNC, past presidents, etc. They are not elected delegates. These super delegates can pledge or withdraw their support for the candidates as they so wish.

This situation was ugly in the 2008 Democratic Party primaries since there was no clear winner among the last two remaining candidates. The battle was between Mr. Barack Obama and Mrs. Hillary Clinton. The battle for support from super delegates was ugly and nasty. They were ugly words spoken, threats, promises for this and that, etc. Super delegates kept switching sides mainly based on unprincipled grounds. In my opinion, keeping changing support by the super delegates showed a lack of seriousness in the task before them. Some people said that they might be using the chance to position themselves in case their party wins the presidential elections. It, therefore, appears as if it is for them other than for the good of the party. Some super delegates were giving surprising reasons for supporting or switching support for a candidate. For instance, some Super Delegates advanced that their daughters, sons, children, wives, family, or friends were responsible for making them to support or change support for a particular candidate. These are not sound reasons for choosing the best candidate for the party. The super delegates are supposed to use their conscience and also consult their constituents in their area, look at the candidate and then zero on the one with the best credentials.

It was wrong for the party to punish elected delegates from Florida and Michigan only because the states decided to vote early so that their choice could have a better say in the election process of their party candidate. These disqualified delegates had better credentials to vote than the ever support switching super delegates.

All these matters must be addressed by the DNC, the States, and Congress where necessary. The DNC should devise a way of giving an opportunity to all states to participate in choosing their party candidate. They could enable them to do this by rotating the order in which States hold their primaries. A rotational basis for holding the primary elections will ensure that Iowa and other states which always vote early and hold a better chance of deciding the presidential candidate of the Democratic Party do not do so in perpetuity.

The Democratic National Congress (DNC) should also address the Super Delegates' issue since 20% of the total delegates as super delegates is too high. The number of elected delegates could be increased so that the impact of super delegates is significantly minimized.

F. CONCLUDING REMARKS

Overall, it is great to note that President Obama must be commended for running a remarkable race. From almost zero-rating to winning the primaries was a miraculous achievement. He rallied the old, the young, the extreme left and right of the Democratic Party to carry the day. He had the press on his side and promised change to America. The support of the Kennedy family who are natural rivals of the Clintons was a great boost to candidate Obama. Many super delegates who had supported Hillary Clinton started defecting slowly towards the Obama camp. The black caucus super delegates had to be part of what was slowly but surely going to produce the first black candidate and they had to be a part of it.

Blaming Bill Clinton was unfair for the remarks he made during the South Carolina primary campaigns period. It was just an excuse, for those who wanted or were under pressure to switch sides. This is because the Nevada primary results had already shown how the election was trending with the black community voting for Barak Obama in large numbers. I do not think that Bill Clinton is a racist nor did he have intentions of racism in his mind when he expressed his opinion about the voting trend in South Carolina. He was portrayed negatively by many people from all walks of life. The truth is that whatever he said could not have stopped the momentum of a voting trend that had already started before the South Carolina primaries.

As for Hilary Clinton, there are many opinions that she did not run such a strategic campaign. That her campaign team took too many things for granted. She was the front runner and nothing would happen to upset her position, so her campaign team thought. They seemed to have planned her campaign in such a way that victory would be hers by Super Tuesday.

A string of losses after Super Tuesday and her statement on Bosnia was devastating. In my case, my political opinions are for free-market principles but this time I did not support the Republicans because they did not have a better candidate than Hillary Clinton. I, therefore, decided to support Hilary Clinton for the presidency because I thought she was the best candidate. By the time I came to that conclusion, Barack Obama was not yet in the picture as a possible presidential candidate. I was always attacked by the black community for supporting her. I did not mind because I had decided to support Hillary Clinton as a matter of principle and I was not likely to change my mind unless there was a good reason for doing so. I was of the opinion that Hillary Clinton would rule from the center like her husband.

There is a tendency for black people, in general, to naturally belong to the Democratic Party. I do not subscribe to that kind of politics. I support candidates who support free-market principles.

I tried to make myself acquainted with the USA political party procedures but I found it hard to be invited by the Clinton local Campaign center. There was a suspicion as to why I wanted to join them. I went once or twice to one of their VA offices to see how I could get an overview of how party politics is conducted in America. What I found was that most of her campaign team seemed to have lost steam. This was not a good sign. In politics, you have to try and try until the end, because fortunes keep shifting all the time.

That is why I commend Hillary for not giving up. She fought till the end and at least showed that although she lost the nomination, she had the popular vote. This should give some thought to the DNC to look at their rules to reflect the will of the voters.

The media tried to influence the outcome of both the party primaries and general elections and to a large extent, they did. The biggest loser was Hilary Clinton. Though she was the front runner, she was battered especially from both the left and right-leaning media. Many pro-Obama people, newspapers, and T.V. commentators were asking her to get out of the way. Even women, who one would think could support a female candidate, were telling her to withdraw. Her husband Bill Clinton, who was once the champion of the minorities, was now called racist and was blamed for using the race card in Georgia. It is a good thing for emerging democracies that she refused to give in to the pressure and insults till the end. This helps to show that in such a close encounter every vote must count. It is common in emerging democracies for candidates to be intimidated and forced to withdraw before the people decide and that is not good for democracy. That is why I was surprised that even President Jimmy Carter the defender of democracy in the emerging democracies was also telling her to get out of the way.

It is important that the system should reflect the intent and will of the people. Influences of the press, TV Networks, party establishments, money, etc. should be minimized so that the democratic process can work well and produce the best results. Nobody should force anyone to get out of the way in favor of their candidate. In this way, the winning candidates will know where the power lies.

CHAPTER 7

OUTSTANDING CONGRESS ISSUES AND SOLUTIONS

By not attending to all these issues raised so far Congress appears to be the weakest link in the struggle to address and find solutions to the people's ever-increasing list of outstanding unsolved problems. Congress should endeavor not to surrender its constitutional duties to the other arms of government because this threatens the very existence of democracy and creates an imbalance in the way the constitution was designed. Congress is supposed to be the main protector of democracy as designed and projected in the constitution. If they abandon this role, the fate of democracy is in jeopardy. The failure of Congress to address the nation's problems has led the general public to lose confidence in the institution. The main problem is that both parties are polarized in their positions and both parties tend to vote as a block regardless of the issues at hand. Congressional representatives were originally designed to vote their conscience over issues and not what their party bosses decide. Congress must therefore look for a way to overcome these deficiencies.

At this juncture we shall move on to discuss, and examine in-depth and recommend courses of action for those other issues which Congress and the Executive have been unable to address and solve because to them, they seem to be politically too hot to handle. It is also important to note that none of the two parties holds any adequate solutions to solve these problems. These issues were mentioned earlier in the book but in this chapter, we try to deal with them in detail. It is only after solving these current problems that other major issues such as tax reform and budget structural reforms can successfully be addressed. If these are all addressed then in the end it will be easier to deal with the ever-growing national debt. In order to avoid party bickering, it is recommended that non-partisan committees be appointed by congress to look at all these issues and recommend solutions. By so doing congress and the executive will avoid the usual blame game by all sorts of people and special interests. If solutions are found and implemented Congress would have done a great favor to the American people by finding solutions to these long outstanding problems.

We begin by mentioning these issues by addressing the entitlement programs first.

100) MEDICAID

100. A) PURPOSE:

This program was created on July 30th, 1965 under the Social Security Act. The purpose of the program was to cater mainly to the following groups:

1. low income and resource groups
2. Pregnant women
3. Children
4. Dentures100.

B) FUNDING:

The program is funded approximately 50% by the State and the other 50% by the Federal Government. Percentages of the federal contributions to the states may vary depending on a number of criteria. The average contribution by the Federal Government to the states could be as high as 57%.

The program has been expanding over the years and the 2010 Patient Protection And Affordable Care Act is likely to increase the Medicaid cost in the coming years as more people are covered by the program. The cost of the program is likely to expand from

USD 118 billion in 2000 to USD 275 billion in 2010 and 487 billion by the year 2020.

When the program was first introduced, it was supposed to serve just a few people but even in the first year alone, it exceeded the original estimate. In 1990 the program served 25million, this increased to 43 million people in the year 2000, and 64 million people in the year 2009. About 16 million more people will be added to the program by the year 2019 because of the 2010 Patient Protection And Affordable Care Act . Additional provisions will bring the total number of people to be served to be over 80 million.

100. C) Scope and Problems of Medicaid

Medicaid covers comprehensive medical coverage including inpatients, hospital stays, doctors' visits, prescription drugs, and nursing home care. This service even encourages people in the higher income bracket to compete for the same. Long-term home nursing care for the elderly takes about 40% of long-term care costs and about 33% of Medicaid costs. The 2010 Patient Protection Act will expand community service assistance and expand the program to all the States. Workers will also be eligible for home care if they become disabled. See.www downsizing government. org/hhs/legislation.

(100Ci). The Federal Government is encouraging the States to expand this program and serve more people so that the States can utilize the stimulus funds as passed by Congress. States have embarked on over-expanding the program so that they can claim more money from the Federal government. As a result, so many unimportant programs have been created and started by the States which under normal circumstances should not have considered as critical to cover. This is especially so for those States who get reimbursement well beyond the average of 57%.

(100Cii). The system, may, as a result, could have encouraged fraud and abuse of the service. According to Congressional Budget Office (CBO), about 10% of the Medicaid money is spent on direct fraud and abuse. According to Harvard University Malcolm

Sparrow, he estimates that fraud and abuse cases are about 20% or 60 billion dollars a year. For states like New York, it is estimated that 10% goes into direct fraud, and another 20-30% more is involved in dubious spending.

(100Ciii). The problem with the program is that it is a huge complex that is lightly policed and therefore easily exploited. The New York Times is said to have reported that there was a dentist who had 991 separate procedures in one day. They are also said to report that there is abuse in transport claims. It is also alleged that criminal gangs steal muscle-building drugs meant for aids patients and this runs in billions. There are other claims that criminal billing of people pretending to be doctors is also a big concern. Double billing by institutions and practitioners has also said to have been detected. These are some of the exploits in the system.

100. D) SOLUTIONS TO MEDICAID

(100Di). It has been observed by various sources that Medicaid and Medicare suffer from many fraud cases. According to some of the various studies, fraud cases from the two programs are in excess of 625 billion dollars over a ten-year period. The country could save this money if fraud cases are closely monitored and treat many more people without budget increments. Presently less than 5% of Medicaid and Medicare claims are audited.

(100Dii). According to Representative Paul Ryan (R-WI), if the country adopted the block grant system for Medicaid funding, as much as 760 billion could be saved. Paul Ryan on his part further suggests that people with long-term conditions could be covered under the proposed block grants funding as no other system might be prepared to take them on at a reasonable cost. Treating long-term condition patients under this system would greatly reduce insurance premiums as many people would take advantage of such an expanded program. President Ronald Reagan and George Bush tried to bring legislation for introducing block grants but in both cases, the matter was not successful. This cost-saving system should now be seriously considered and implemented as a matter of urgency. The Block Grant system if adopted together with a tax credit and voucher system would eliminate unnecessary agencies that have been overseeing the current Medicaid system. This is because the individual beneficiaries would be the ones with the responsibility to pay. The system would work like what is done with food stamps. Other people reason that the system would be difficult to police. It is however still worth looking at it more critically and sees where improvements can be made.

Some people further suggest that if the Federal Government gave grants to the States then the program would work within affordable budgetary limits as the States would be aware of the funding levels they would be working with. Another advantage is that this will force States to pursue cost-saving measures and innovations without compromising healthcare standards. It will also force the States to control frauds, abuse through unnecessary spending because the present unlimited claims system would be eliminated. Presently, the program is controlled by the States and the Federal government has no say on how e the States can expand the program. All these cost-saving measures can keep the programs viable and solvent most likely without increase the budget, but most probably with less budgeting spending. It is therefore important that the Medicaid program gets an urgent overhaul. Many more people could be treated within the same spending.

It is my belief that part of the funds saved from the above changes would be used to cover the medical cost of the more 30 million uninsured people who are unable to afford insurance. There is no reason why healthcare treatment should be tied to healthcare insurance without which people cannot get treatment.

101) MEDICARE

This social program was created in 1965. The program has been amended over the years and now covers the following:

101A) PART A OF MEDICARE

It covers up to 80% of the cost for people 65 years old and above in the following areas:

i) Hospital in-patient stays including room and board, Doctors' fees, etc.

ii) It caters to people with long-term kidney diseases, no matter what age.

iii) It caters to the disabled who cannot work.

iv) It caters to residency training programs for most physicians in the USA.

101B) PART B

This covers 75% medical insurance for outpatients including physicians and nursing services, X-rays, lab diagnosis, etc.

101C) PART C

This covers the Medicare advantage prescription plan.

101D) PART D

This covers 75% of prescription drug plan for the elderly.

Part B and D are administered by the social security administration. Part A and B are eligible to participate in part D.

In the year 2009 Medicare program attended to 46.3 million people.

101E) FUNDING MEDICARE

The program is funded mainly by the payroll tax. The employees contribute 1.4 5% of their emoluments and the employer contributes a similar percentage making a total contribution of 2.9%. In the year 2013, single filers earning over $ 200,000 a year and joint income tax filers earning over $250,000 per annum will be required to contribute to the fund an extra 0.9 % of their earnings.

In the year 2009, over 160 million taxpayers subscribed to this program. According to the Board of Trustees for social security and Medicare annual report of 2010, the program is likely to exhaust its funds by the year 2029. After that year the collection will likely finance up to 85% of the required expenditure. This will go down to 76% of the required expenditure by the year 2045, rising to 89% by the year 2084. There is therefore a need to make adjustments in the program by raising it from the current 1.9% Gross Domestic Product (GDP) to 3.5% of GDP by the year 2040 in order to cover the projected shortfalls.

102) Social Security

This is an insurance program that was created in 1935.

102A) Purpose

The purpose of the program mainly covers the following:

Federal Retirement Benefits and also death plus survivor benefits.

It covers disability insurance

Unemployment benefits

Medicare part B and D

Temporary assistance to needy families

Social security is the largest single government program accounting for 20.8% of government expenditure. The program for the time being currently supports budget and public expenditure because all surplus money is by statute used to purchase government securities.

Since 1990 social security net annual positions do no longer form part of the budget but are included in the unified budget. However, still CBO gives figures for both scenarios first without off-budget items and those which include the off-budget items.

See ref. www.ssa.gov/history/budgettreatment.html.

In 2004 the deficit of the USA budget was U$ 412 billion including the off-budget items and if excluded the deficit was U$ 567 billion.

102B) Funding

Social security is funded by payroll through FICA and by the self-employed through SECA. FICA is charged at 5.3% of employee salary and 5.3% contribution by the employer making the total rate 10.6 %. In addition, the employee pays 0.9% disability insurance and the employer contributes the same making a total contribution of 1.8 as disability insurance. In 2010 there was a cap of USD 106,800 and so no charge was and is levied over this amount. All collections from the above two funds are held in the OASDI fund. The OASDI fund, therefore, represents old age and survives insurance retirement benefits and disability insurance benefits.

102C) Status

The present status of the social security fund is as follows:

i. Over 150 million people contribute to the fund. ii. Social security expenditure in 2010 will exceed tax receipt for the first time since 1983. The reason for this shortfall is due to a US$ 25 billion downward adjustment and the current recession which has reduced social security receipts because many people lost their jobs. However, this trend is likely to be reversed by the year 2012-2014. The pressure on social security expenses will again pick up in the year 2015 as the baby boomers will start collecting their social security benefits. (See 2010 annual report by the social security Medicare boards of trustees. See ref: www.ssa.gov/oact/trsum/index.html

This substantial rise in the numbers of beneficiaries after 2015 as a result of the baby boom generation who will be at that time eligible for retirement in large numbers will again make expenditures begin to rise and most likely shoot above the fund receipts.

The trustees, therefore, recommend action to be taken sooner rather than later to solve the long-term financial challenges facing social security and Medicare programs. They project that the OASDI trust fund will be exhausted by the year 2044 and they reckon that the program will spend 6.4% of the Gross Domestic Product (GDP) by the year 2084. They also project that the Disability Insurance Fund will be exhausted by the year 2018. The combined funds of the two funds will be exhausted by the year 2037. (See chart B of SSA annual report ref. income and cost rates). The Congressional Budget Office (CBO) however projects depletion of these funds by the year 2052. After funds are depleted it is projected that the Social Security fund receipts will be able to finance about 76% of the projected budget.

CHART B—INCOME AND COST RATES

(Percentage of taxable payroll)

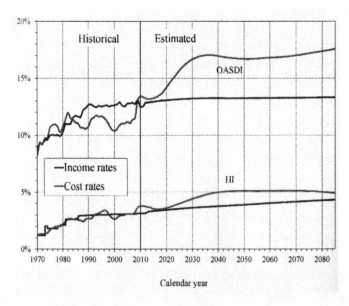

There is definitely a funding problem for Social Security Fund which needs urgent attention. Those who think it is a serious matter recommend that something should be done quickly. President

Bush in his address to the nation on February 2nd, 2005, warned that Social Security was heading to bankruptcy if nothing was done immediately. However Nobel Laureate economist, Paul Kurgan while acknowledging that there is a long-run financing problem, he is of the opinion that it is not as severe but modest in size. Some people sight that the Congress Budget Office (CBO) proposal of 0.54% increases in GDP contribution to the fund will be able to address the problem of Social Security. Others contend that the shortfall is less than 3% of the budget and only a fraction of the Bush Tax cuts of those people earning over half a million dollars per annum. They further contend that this shortfall can therefore be met if those earning more than half a million dollars can pay a little more extra. This can be looked at and see the wisdom of such action. The main question with the above idea is whether a few people should be taxed to cover the shortfalls of a collection fund.

102D) SUMMARY OF POSSIBLE SOLUTIONS
TO ADDRESS SOCIAL SECURITY

Many solutions have been suggested to address Social Security challenges and the following are among some of them:

(i) To remove the $106,800 cap from FICA payments

(ii) Increase the retirement years because people are living longer

(iii) Introduction of private or partial private accounts

(iv) Mr. Greenspan is reported to have suggested that there are only three choices for social fund reform namely: raise taxes, lower benefits, or bail out the program by tapping general revenue. They further state that Mr. Greenspan is of the opinion that the easiest political choice is by a stroke of a pen and printing money. (See. Ref:www.nytimes.com/2010/03/25/business/economy/25social.html)/.

ADVANTAGES AND DISADVANTAGES

Here are some of the advantages and disadvantages of the above proposals:

102DI) REMOVAL OF OASDI PAY TAX CAPS

As regards the removal of all Old Age, Survivors and Disability Insurance Program (OASDI) payroll tax cap on $106,800 per annum as of 2010 for those FICA taxpayers, many people argue that restricting or placing caps favors the rich as they don't have to pay taxes for any earning above that amount. This is in contrast to the lower-income groups who pay taxes on all of what they earn. Others however argue that since the rich do not normally get back all the money that they contribute, the cap should stay. Some still argue that since there are no restrictions on HI fund collections, the same should apply to FICA as well and therefore the cap should not be there. They also argue that richer people tend to live longer and therefore are likely to benefit more years from the fund than other contributors who don't normally live that long. They further argue that keeping caps makes the system to be regressive. According to Nobel Laureate economist, Milton Friedman, he thinks that the Social Security Fund system redistributes wealth from the poor to the wealthy due to the present limitation.

According to the American Association of Retired Persons (AARP) study, if the cap was raised to 90% of the earnings, there would be approximately a 39% reduction in the shortfall of the social security fund problem. According to another study, the above measure will affect only approximately 6% of the working population. This would create a more progressive tax and reduce the deficit, by 39% as already mentioned.

102 DII) INCREASE RETIREMENT AGE

According to the same AARP study, an increase in the retirement age to 70 years would result in a 36% reduction in the shortfall of the fund. However, the effect of this alternative is that:

It links the whole scheme to life expectancy.

It is unfair for those forced to retire early but not eligible for Social Security benefits.

It denies the economy from hiring younger people who are desirous of getting into the job market

102 Dɪɪɪ) Private Accounts

Center on budget and policy priorities estimated that President Bush's 2005 privatization proposal would increase the federal debt by USD 1 trillion in the first decade and USD 3.5 trillion in the decade thereafter. This is because privatization of the fund would separate

Social Security from the budget and national debt. At the moment all surplus collections from the fund must buy securities and the money is used by the government to pay for its programs. The interest rate of return from securities is approximately 2.9%.

Many people argue that the whole concept is therefore not about how to benefit the individual taxpayer but to benefit Uncle Sam. If we get out of this concept, then rational decisions can be made about how to maximize benefits for those who contribute to the fund.

Many of those in favor of private accounts would prefer partial to whole privatization of the fund So that the fund is invested in a basket of options. Private accounts which would be invested under these options and are better illustrated by the Galveston county model for social security (see. Ref: www.unitypublishing.com/ government/galveston social security plan.html.

The Galveston County Private Accounts System started in 1981 when the county opted out of the Social Security Fund system. Based on retirement after 30 years of service, it is believed that the Galveston workers would be better off as under based on different salary structures:—

i) Workers making $17,000 per annum would make approximately 50% higher per month under the county system i.e. US$1036 versus $683 under the social security fund system respectively. Those making US$26,000 pa would make almost 100% higher or US$1500 versus US$853 pm. Those making US$51000pa could make US$3103 versus US$1368 pm. Those who earn US$75000 pa earn US$4540pm versus US$1645 pm.

ii) Survivors Benefits: Galveston County also offers more as Compared To Social Security. Under the county program, workers get between $75,000 and $215,000 versus social security where the survivors must wait until the workers are 60 years old to qualify for 75% of the workers' wages.

Other sources however argue that Social Security benefits are better than the Galveston county model for the lower-income earners especially if they live longer. They claim that those workers who live longer could draw more than what they put in the fund.

Since what matters is to get maximum benefits for the workers and as figures from Galveston county look attractive, there would be no harm in using a percentage of the workers' contribution to the fund for investing in these private accounts. In any case, Galveston County invested the county's funds in a guaranteed fixed rate annuity with an average return of 6.5%. There is a saying in my tribe that where there is food, milk, etc the baby should not be left to cry. Don't ask just give the baby the food and there will be no crying. The money is there and it belongs to the workers. Let congress make the necessary changes to allow the private accounts to be tried out. Congress should not block this opportunity which could benefit the workers. There is also another saying that the taste of the pudding is in the eating. The private accounts option should not be blocked but should be tried out. Lame excuses for delaying or denying what looks to be an attractive proposal should no longer be entertained.

102 DIV) Suggested changes
regarding social security fund

Some people suggest that surpluses from the fund should also be invested in other areas other than buying only government securities. They also suggested that part of the current social security fund savings held in government securities should also be divested into other investments. The following investment options have been floated:

(1) Capital Markets:
Part of the money in the fund can be Invested can under a guaranteed rate of return. This would be based on the same kind of lines as that of the Galveston system.

(2)Investing in Property :
Part of the investments can be put in the housing industry. The fund can be used to construct, buy, rent and sell houses and commercial properties for the benefit of the workers. This would as result encourage more competition in the housing industry and marketing. The value of the fund would also be protected by the ownership of the redeemable tangible assets.

(3) The rest of the money can be left in government securities investments as is already being done now.

(4) The fund managers would also be charged to look for other viable investment opportunities not mentioned above. The main idea and goal should be to invest the workers' money into a variety of options which gives workers better returns on their savings. This will reap maximum benefits for the workers when they retire. The Galveston illustration is a clear example. This will also reduce government dependence on Social Security Fund surpluses to finance government projects, which indirectly and artificially hides the position of the national debt.

At the moment all surpluses have been used by the government to finance government projects and when the time comes to redeem these investments the same taxpayers will be taxed more to pay the fund holders. This is because the government has used the money to finance budgetary and project demands over the years. The alternative to increased taxation would be for the government to just print more money and pay. This would have its own complications on the economy such as fueling inflation and devaluation of the currency in the long run.

It is not fair for the workers by those people who do not believe that maximizing returns on the fund investments should be the primary consideration. They want to make the fund just secure and not necessarily profitable.

However, even in the bible, there is the parable of the rich man who distributed talents to his servants before he left for a business trip far away in the country. He gave five talents to one servant, two talents to the second, and one talent to the third one. When he returned the one who was given five talents had doubled them to ten and the one who was given two had also doubled his to four. Unfortunately, the one who was given one talent had buried in the ground for fear of losing the money and mistrust of his master. He indeed did not make any profit and was severely punished. As a country, we should also emulate the example of this parable and try to maximize returns on the investments for those who entrust their money with the government or any other scenario.

I too have my own experience with the social security fund in Uganda where I originally come from. The government set up a social security fund in 1965. I contributed 5% of my salary and my employer contributed a similar percentage. When I resigned from my employment I had saved up to the equivalent of US$10,000 in the fund. When I recently qualified to draw from the fund to my surprise and disappointment the value of my account was only Uganda shillings 20,000 which at the current rate of exchange at UG Shs.2, 200 to US$1, the value in dollar terms of my investment was less than US$10. This is because when I invested the exchange rate was about Uganda. Shs.7.5 to the dollar. Had they invested my money into tangible assets or even kept my money in an external currency holding account, I would not have lost the money I had saved. I did not even bother about the U$ 10 because it is not worth struggling for.

In Zimbabwe, it is even a worse scenario because of hyperinflation. The situation there is so bad that almost every citizen is a billionaire. One needs billions of Zimbabwe dollars to go shopping in the market. It would appear that in Zimbabwe it is not just a dream but for real to be a billionaire. This reminds me of Travie McCoy's billionaire Ft song where one would dream of appearing on the cover of Forbes Magazine if one became a billionaire and smile with celebrities. In Zimbabwe, it is the norm. When Zimbabwe became independent the value of its currency was 1.47 Zimbabwe dollars to 1 US dollar. Now the value of the Zimbabwe dollar is hovering around 600,000 Zimbabwe dollars to 1 US dollar. People who were holding the local Zimbabwe currency in cash or deposits have lost badly because of Mugabe's government's bad policies.

There are reports that people in Zimbabwe are now allowed to use other convertible currencies, such as US dollars, pounds, etc while transacting business because the Zimbabwe dollar is so unpredictable.

I have brought up the above examples to illustrate the extremes of what can happen to investments if bad decisions are made. Because of the relative stability of the US dollar, people may not see clearly the concept of maximizing returns on investments.

Conclusions Social Security Fund

There are concerns over the future of the Social Security Fund. In fact, Social security appears to be having fewer problems than the other entitlement programs. If one or two or several of the above-mentioned solutions or any other are adopted it is possible that the funding problem of the fund can be easily addressed. What is required is political will by Congress to address and solve the matter in a non-partisan manner. The main concern with the fund is that the money has actually been borrowed to fund other government programs with minimal returns

103) Health Care Reform

Healthcare and Education Reconciliation Act of 2010

The fourth entitlement program is health care as amended recently by the 2010 Health Care And Education Reconciliation Act.

103A) Background

The Health Care And Education Reconciliation Act of 2010 which amended the Patient Protection And Affordable Care Act of 2010 was signed in law on March 30th, 2010. The act made a wide range of changes in the health care industry. There was a lot of fierce debating while the act was being discussed partly because neither the Republicans nor the Democrats were willing to listen to one another. They were not willing to make any compromises, concessions in order to produce an all-inclusive pro-American health care act containing all possible suggestions and solutions for the good and benefit of the American people. Health care reform is a very vital component of the American population and should have been handled beyond party line considerations. Because the act was considered with narrow parochial interests it has not been wholly accepted by the majority of the general public and is still facing a lot of opposition while being implemented. The health care bill became a victim of bickering by the two parties. On top of that, the bill was introduced in Congress for debate, without first listening to all possible ideas and suggestions. While the Democrats should take the blame for not sharing ideas with others, the Republicans also share part of the blame. When the Republicans lost the 2008 elections and the Democrats took both the presidency and congress, they embarked on a program to disorganize the democrats. The Republicans went full blast to see how they could regain power. They, therefore, decided to literary oppose almost everything the Democrats brought on the floor for debate. They came to be known as the "NO" party.

Indeed their chance came when the Democrats miss-timed and introduced the controversial health care reform bill on the floor without having made enough preparation and political strategy. The Democratic Party leadership seems not to have made enough consultation among their fellow democrats. They did not try to woo enough Republicans to support the bill and make it appear to be a bi-partisan effort. They also did not have enough interaction with other stakeholders and most importantly the population. The Republicans were most likely surprised to see the Democrats bring something like that to them on a silver platter. The Republicans immediately pounced onto this chance and punched as many holes as they possibly could to make the bill unpopular as much as possible, especially among the population. The Republicans were lucky because the majority of the population was also against many of the provisions of the health care bill. Another main problem was that many people did not understand the bill because it was not well explained and popularized before it was tabled for debate in congress. What is important to note is that the Republicans did not either have a comprehensive solution to health care themselves. Many people have been wondering why the republicans did not tackle the problem themselves when of late they have been in power for more years than the Democrats. It is only the Democrats under President Clinton and Obama who at least made attempts to solve the health care problem which was experiencing soaring costs and they should at least be commended for trying.

One also wonders why the democrats brought the controversial health care bill so hurriedly. It appears that after winning the 2008 elections, things were going so well that the Democrats were not enthusiastic about listening to anybody. They came to be known as the "I KNOW" party. They were always reminding everyone how they had won the mandate of the people in 2008. They thought that it was their turn to be listened to. Every time the Republicans raised a voice, the Democrats reminded them of how they were losers and had been rejected by people and they reasoned that the Republicans in the first place had put the country in the current mess.

Therefore in summary:

The Democratic leadership did not sell the bill to their fellow Democrats in Congress before tabling it for debate. This is why there was a division within the ranks of the Democratic Party, mainly between the left-wing radicles and the blue dogs. There are some suggestions that the bill was drafted by the left-wing of the Democratic Party and that they did not consult the blue dogs for ideas so that they also would go along with the bill. Many of the representatives in both houses were not even aware of the provisions in the bill and could not properly respond or interpret the bill when being interviewed by journalists and other media network representatives.

ii. The Democrats did not either sell the bill to the Republicans or entertain contributions from them. The bill, therefore, became the property of the Democratic Party, and not Congress as a whole.

iii. Most importantly they did not sell the bill to the general public. This is one of the reasons why so many senior citizens and independents who had previously voted for the Democratic Party switched to the Republican Party during the midterm November 2010 elections. In fact, the Democratic Party machinery had attacked anybody who made any criticism of the bill especially the Tea Party goers. For shouting down and calling all sorts of bad names to anybody who was critical of the bill, especially the Tea Party goers, the Democratic Party paid a high price during the 2010 midterm elections. One lady warned and told the Democrats that they had woken up a sleeping giant. During the 2010 midterm elections the Republicans used health care repeal as one of their campaign tools and it paid off. The Republicans regained the House of Representatives with a net gain of 63 seats and also reduced the deficit in the Senate by 8 seats.

The Health Care and Education Reconciliation Act of 2010 was eventually passed. It is said that the Democrats used everything at their disposal including intimidation, persuasion, incentives, political favors, backhand maneuvers and they had also to use the nuclear option in the Senate when the bill had run into a stalemate.

103(B). PROBLEMS OF THE HEALTH CARE ACT

The Act has run into the following problems since it became law. It has so many controversial provisions and omissions. The following are some of the controversies:

i) It has been challenged in court by more than 29 states, organizations, and individuals on the grounds that the act contains unconstitutional provisions. The main complaint is that it forces people to buy a product that infringes upon the basic rights of the individual. There is a provision that implies that if a person refuses to buy medical care insurance, a fine imposed upon that individual.

ii) Over 1000 companies and organizations have been given concessions since the act has been enacted because they were unable to provide cheap insurance to their employees under the new healthcare act. The requirements of the new act would have considerably increased insurance costs. Making these provisions on a selective basis means that the ground is no longer leveled. This is an animal farm at work. The Act also exempts trade unions and teacher associations from complying with some of these and other provisions. The act, therefore, needs further review in order to make it equitable for all the players.

iii) The act is too big and therefore contains a lot of superfluous provisions which should be removed. It should not be the government's business to micro-manage private business. Many of those dos and don'ts should be eliminated from the act because it is not government business to tell the insurance or any other business how they should conduct their business. Furthermore, it is not easy for ordinary folk and even learned people to read, digest, understand and interpret such an amorphous document. The size of the act is equivalent to about ten novels which would take some time for an ordinary person to read. On top of that one has to take into account that the act is a technical document. The act also requires one to read a lot of references and therefore it takes time to really understand every clause. For a technical document, every sentence and clause has a lot of complications and implications. One can therefore imagine the number of man-hours that would be needed to dissect and understand the act.

iv) New controversial implications of the act are being discovered and revealed almost on a daily basis. The latest to the surface was that US dollar 105 billion that was authorized to be spent by the Secretary for Health without referral to Congress. Many Members of Congress are now surprised and dismayed with what they voted for. The House of Representatives has since attempted to block this expenditure but it seems the democratic majority in the Senate will block this attempt. The Republicans, who won the majority in the House of Representatives during the 2010 midterm elections, also went ahead and passed a resolution repealing the Health Care and Education Reconciliation Act. However, this measure is also unlikely to pass beyond the Democratic-controlled Senate.

103 (C) Conclusions

(a) It is therefore important that this act should be reviewed by all stakeholders including Members of Congress, the Executive, insurance companies, the states, trade unions, health care providers, hospitals, Christian organizations, and peoples' representatives at all levels only to mention but a few of the possible participants. Good provisions in the Act should be retained. Good provisions from the Republican Party and those from the general public and other sources should also be included in the revised act. Those matters should be debated with the idea of hammering out a long-term but easy-to-understand pro-American people health care act.

(b) It was sad to politicize this important issue and push it down the peoples' throats because the act has now become a poisoned pill. There is now a need to remove the contaminated parts of the act, add new ones but retain the good ones, and come out with a solution acceptable by the people. Congress should also look at the good provisions used by healthcare providers in other countries and adopt those which are good for the American system.

103(D) SOME OBSERVATIONS AND SOLUTIONS TO HEALTH CARE(1).

The following observations have been made regarding the healthcare system in the USA as compared to those providers in other developed countries: According to www.en.wikipedia.org/wiki/health-care-in-theunited-state, website observes that:

a) Health care in the USA is provided by many legal entities.

b) Health care facilities in the USA are largely operated by private sectors through private health care insurance. The exceptions are Medicare, Medicaid, Tri-care, the children's health care insurance program, and the veterans' health administration.

c) The US census mentions that a record number of 50.7 million Americans or 16.7 % of the population were without medical insurance as of the end of 2009. The above figure is said to include 9.9 million non-citizens.

d) The USA spends more money on healthcare per person than any other country in the world.

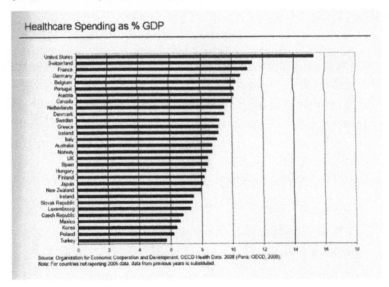

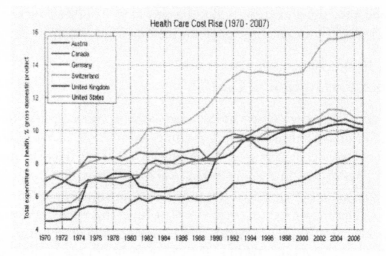

Health Care Cost Rise (1970 - 2007)

See charts above... ref www.en.wikipedia.org/wiki/
list_of-countries_by_total_health_expenditure_ppp.

This information is provided by the organization for economic cooperation and development (OECD) comprising of the 30 industrialist countries and WHO

e) Medical debt accounts for 46.2% of personal bankruptcies in the USA.

f) Other sources:—other sources also indicate that

(i). Premiums up by 78% from 2001 to 2007 wages 19% study by Kaiser family complete

(ii). Less than 9% of the population purchase individual health care insurance.

(iii). Allegations of waste by Dr. Donald Berwick once the Administrator of the Centers of Medicare and Medicaid services asserted that 20% to 30% of healthcare spending goes to waste due to the following.

(a) Over treatment of patients

(b) Failure to coordinate healthcare

(c) Administrative complexity of the healthcare system.

(d) Burdensome rules

(e) Fraud

(iv). In 2004 private insurance paid for 36% of personal healthcare expenditures Federal Government paid 34% local government 11% out of pocket private expenditure accounted for 15% while other private funds accounted for 4%

(v). Although the Emergency Medical Treatment and Active Labor Act requires virtually all hospitals to accept all patients for emergency room treatment, there is no provision for preventive or continuity of treatment, those who cannot afford healthcare costs or insurance are left in Limbo. Although 84.7% of the population is covered by some sort of insurance, there are many gray areas not covered by some of the insurance policies. Some of these include long-term treatment.

(vi). In 2004 the institute of medicine recommended, through a study that the nation should implement a strategy to achieve universal insurance healthcare coverage. It is worth noting that most of the studies use insurance as the only alternative towards universal healthcare coverage in the USA. As if nothing can be done without involving insurance.

(2). From the above information the following implications can be noted ;

i. There are serious concerns by many people as to why people in the USA should not have a right to health care access as is in so many other less endowed countries. Here we should observe that the declaration of independence talks about life as one of the fundamentals to be enjoyed by the people. Providing healthcare to everyone is therefore a fundamental issue that should not be overlooked. Health care should be taken by governments as seriously as the departments of education and defense. When it comes to health care, the government should stop screaming about how it is going to bankrupt the country and find solutions to providing this service. The government has never said how the defense is going to bankrupt the country.

ii. It is doubtful whether the people are getting full value for what they are paying for. This is important since in the USA people pay almost twice as much for health care compared to the other OECD countries and yet at the same time the USA lags behind in such measures as infant mortality, life expectancy and does not provide universal health coverage. The USA for instance is ranked forty-second worldwide in life expectancy and lags behind the G5 nations who also provide full health care coverage.

iii. It should be noted under the same ref as above that US Citizens spent US $8,047 dollars per person for health care in 2009. This being about 53% more than any other industrialized country and 17.3% of GDP. The main possible reasons for these situations are as follows:

iv. DELAY leading to waiting lists. There are supply constraints that create waiting lists in some other countries. Waiting time for non-emergency medical procedures seems to be more serious in some Organization for Economic Co-operation and Development (OECD) countries such as Canada, UK, and Australia. However, some Organization for Economic Co-operation and Development (OECD) countries who also provide universal health care coverage such as Sweden, Switzerland, etc. do not experience these delays. Therefore this does not make the USA have a monopoly over little time waiting for non-emergency procedures. It is a problem that can be reviewed and rectified.

v. Higher incomes and spending. Although US incomes are higher than many other countries, there is no good justification for spending as a percentage of GDP more than the other OECD countries that moreover provide health care for the whole population.

vi. The USA pays more for pharmaceuticals than other industrialized countries for no apparent good justification.

vii. The USA pays more for hospital stays and physician visits. For instance, a day's hospital stays in the USA in the year was US

$2,434 dollars compared to US $870 dollars in Canada and even less in other OECD countries. Even adjusting for higher incomes and cost of living in the USA these amounts are still considerably far apart.

The level of malpractice litigations and defensive medicine practices is high in the USA. Malpractice payments in the USA are growing at a rate of more than 5% above inflation. Net payments for malpractice cases, therefore, keep growing. See http:www. wikipidia.org/wiki/us_tort_reformates, it has been claimed that Frivolous lawsuits drive up healthcare costs and force medical staff at all levels to practice defensive medicine which leads to many unnecessary referrals which are costly and wasteful. Doctors, nurses, and other medical personnel they say tend to focus less on health and more on possible liability claims. It is reasoned that medical practitioners will practice with less fear if excessive malpractice suits are not hanging over their necks. According to a study published in 2005 in a journal by the American Medical Association, 93% of physicians surveyed reported practicing defensive medicine or altering chemical behavior because of the threat of malpractice liability. Of those surveyed, 43% reported using digital imaging technology in clinically unnecessary circumstances. These included MRIs and CAT Scans.

The trial lawyers on the other hand dispute these figures. They state that the malpractice lawsuits represent a small portion which is no more than 3% of the health care expenditure costs. They also claim that savings on defensive medicine are exaggerated.

There is therefore a big gap in estimates of what defensive cost savings could be. The trial lawyers say it is very negligible. Congressional Budget Office (CBO) on the other hand estimates that it is in the region of 50 billion dollars a year and other estimates put the figure as high as 200 billion dollars a year in savings. As the saying goes that the proof of the pudding is in the eating, it can only be found out after it has been tried out. There is therefore a very good case for this idea to be part of the healthcare act.

The main changes advocated for tort reform include litigations on punitive damages, non-economic damages, collateral source doctrine, appeal bond requirements, only to mention but a few.

103D) OTHER POSSIBLE SOLUTIONS TO HEALTH CARE

The main aim of the USA should be to provide the best health care for all its residents at the lowest possible cost. The following link will show the full extent of how the US fairs compared to the rest of the health care providers: See www.en.wikipedia.org.wiki/list_of_countries_by_total_healthexpenditure_ppp. By OECD (Organization for Economic Cooperation and Development) and WHO (World Health Organization).

The OECD countries are able to provide health care for all for nearly half the cost. There is a good reason for the USA to adopt the good measures used in the 0ECD countries.

LIST OF COUNTRIES BY TOTAL HEALTH EXPENDITURE (PPP) PER CAPITA

OECD (2009)[1]				WHO (2008)[2]			
Rank	Country	Total health expenditure per capita PPP US$	Total health expenditure % of GDP	Rank	Country	Total health expenditure per capita PPP Int.$	Total health expenditure % of GDP
1	United States	7,960	17.4	1	United States	7,164	15.2
2	Norway	5,352	9.6	2	Monaco	5,996	3.6
3	Switzerland	5,144	11.4	3	Luxembourg	5,750	6.8
4	Netherlands	4,914	12.0	4	Norway	5,207	8.5
5	Luxembourg	4,808	7.8	5	Switzerland	4,815	10.7
6	Canada	4,363	11.4	6	Netherlands	4,283	9.9
7	Denmark	4,348	11.5	7	Austria	4,150	10.2
8	Austria	4,289	11.0	8	Belgium	4,096	11.1
9	Germany	4,218	11.6	9	Germany	3,922	10.5
10	France	3,978	11.8	10	Canada	3,867	9.8
11	Belgium	3,946	10.9	11	France	3,851	11.2
12	Ireland	3,781	9.5	12	Denmark	3,814	9.9
13	Sweden	3,722	10.0	13	Ireland	3,797	8.7
14	Iceland	3,538	9.7	14	San Marino	3,690	7.1
15	Australia	3,445 (2008)	8.7 (2008)	15	Sweden	3,622	9.4
16	United Kingdom	3,487	9.8	16	Iceland	3,583	9.2
17	Finland	3,226	9.2	17	Australia	3,365	8.5
18	Italy	3,137	9.5	18	Finland	3,299	8.8
19	Spain	3,067	9.5	19	United Kingdom	3,222	8.7
20	Japan	2,878 (2008)	8.5 (2008)	20	Andorra	3,128	7.5
21	Greece	2,724 (2007)	9.6 (2007)	21	Greece	3,010	10.1
22	New Zealand	2,983	10.3	22	Spain	2,941	9.0
23	Portugal	2,508 (2008)	10.1 (2008)	23	Italy	2,836	8.7

24	Slovenia	2,579	9.3		24	Japan	2,817	8.3
25	Israel	2,104	7.9		25	New Zealand	2,655	9.7
26	Czech Republic	2,108	6.8		26	Portugal	2,578	10.6
27	Slovakia	2,084	9.1		27	Slovenia	2,420	8.3
28	Korea, South	1,879	6.9		28	Niue	2,360	13.5
29	Hungary	1,511	7.4		29	Israel	2,093	8.0
30	Poland	1,394	7.4		30	Taiwan (Republic of China)[3]	2,080	6.5
31	Estonia	1,393	7.0		31	Slovakia	1,849	8.0
32	Chile	1,186	8.4		32	Cyprus	1,838	6.0
33	Turkey	902 (2008)	6.1 (2008)		33	Singapore	1,833	3.3
34	Mexico	918	6.4		34	Czech Republic	1,830	7.1
					35	Korea, South	1,806	6.5
					36	Bahamas, The	1,737	7.2
					37	Qatar	1,691	2.0
					38	Malta	1,664	7.3
					39	Croatia	1,553	7.8
					40	Hungary	1,506	7.2
					41	Barbados	1,498	6.7
					42	Estonia	1,325	6.1
					43	Lithuania	1,318	6.8
					44	Bahrain	1,282	3.7
					45	Poland	1,271	7.0
					46	Trinidad and Tobago	1,237	4.7
					47	Latvia	1,206	6.6
					48	Montenegro	1,162	8.4
					49	Brunei	1,131	2.3
					50	Chile	1,088	7.5

There are many suggestions for solving the healthcare problems among which are the following:

i) Review Costings: It is important for the USA to review prices paid for their health care and try to reduce these costs

ii) Review costing: It is important for the USA to review prices paid for their health care and try to make savings where possible or at least try to reduce these costs and bring them in line with other developed countries. If this can be done the GDP percentage spent on health care could be brought down by 5% and over.

iii) Allow competition among medical drugs suppliers:

There is a need to find out if there is a cartel among health care service providers that keeps prices going up every year. To break any possible collusion it would make economic sense if the USA allowed the importation of medicines from other countries such as Canada Europe etc since they have proved to be cheaper and of comparable quality to the USA medicines. This would bring the prices of medicines down to their true market prices. This policy would be in line with the concept of the free market system that the USA believes in and keeps advocating. The USA should not shift goalposts whenever it is convenient and beneficial to some special interests. There is no good reason why the pharmaceutical industries in the USA should not compete with other drug providers worldwide. This move alone would lessen the heavy burden of medical drug costs imposed on the people's pockets.

It is a bad policy to please medicine manufacturers and sellers at the expense of the people. The reason being given that US medicines are of a higher quality than that of other countries cannot be justified. Not everyone wants to drive a Cadillac, Ferrari, or one of these expensive cars. Other vehicles such as the Japanese, Korean, European car models are just as good as the American models except they are cheaper to buy and maintain. The same should happen with medicines. Let the people decide on what are the best medical drugs suited for them. This is what they do for products like cars and trucks etc. People go shopping for the vehicle that best suits their needs and pocket and it does not matter where the car was manufactured from. In the case of medicine, all the government has to do is to put out basic requirements and standards the drug makers should maintain and produce.

(iv) Allow competition in the health care industry.

The fact is that the private sector plays a major role in providing health care in the USA. However, the system, which is supposed to be more efficient than the public system, has on the contrary proved to be more expensive in providing health care services to the public. This is because the USA spends 53% more on health care than the OECD countries.

The OECD countries have similar standards and economic development to that of the USA. They, therefore, provide good comparisons while discussing healthcare alternatives, costs, and standards. Therefore it would make a lot of sense and would be prudent to allow other systems to compete alongside the private sector systems in providing health care services to the people. In any case, presently there are some programs in the USA running along with the private healthcare providers. These include Medicare, Medicaid, Tricare, and the veterans' healthcare administration, etc. Other types of healthcare alternatives should be allowed to operate.

(v) Reform of the present insurance delivery system:
The following are some of the necessary changes:

(a) Remove unnecessary restrictions from the 2010 health care act and allow private insurance provides function with greater flexibility.

(b) Include new good ideas for health care reforms such as those proposed by Representative Paul Ryan. His ideas include a consumer-driven system based on individual vouchers and tax credits. Under the plan tax credits and a voucher of up to 5000 dollars would give a total of 11000 dollars for a family and 5000 dollars for a single person. Paul Ryan thinks this is a great cost-saving idea because it allows people to choose the best insurance system which best fits their needs. This is a good idea because the young energetic persons may not have the same insurance needs as those of the elderly. His ideas could be amalgamated with good provisions from the present act, and any other new innovations. Provisions in the present health care ACT such as the pre-existing conditions and free medical for children should stay. The main aim should be to provide the cheapest best insurance options. There are other suggestions that can be discussed and incorporated. What is needed is to open up the act for Review and amendment.

(vi) Reform the Health care structure :

It has been suggested by some people that Medicaid, Medicare, and the 2010 Health care Act should be coordinated under one administration. This move will eliminate many unnecessary agencies and streamline the confusion and overlaps within the system. It will also provide a one-stop center for most of the health care requirements and solutions. These programs have been put in place in a haphazard manner and could be reviewed and rationalized so that services are not duplicated and dealt with by many agencies. They may not need to create so many extra agencies as provided in the 2010 health care Act unless the act is amended. This move should end up being a cost-saving measure. The only exception which should be looked into is the disability insurance contributions under the FICA social security arrangements. It may not be possible to transfer this particular program under the above umbrella because of legal and administrative complications.

(vii) Encourage New cost-saving innovations and new ideas
Encourage competition, provide financing and reward those who are responsible for the creation and implementation of new ideas. We could end up with new cost-saving ideas beyond our dreams, for the federal and state government institutions, plus the private sector. Proposals such as using experienced and expert doctors to pass on their expertise using TV, audio, and other innovations to provide medical solutions to the general public can be tried out. Of course, these doctors can arrange a way of being renumerated by those using their programs. Robots etc are now being used to perform quite a number of tasks with unbelievable precision. All these new ideas can make medical expenses more affordable for people.

(viii) Implement Block Grants Idea

If Representative Paul Ryan's idea of block grants for Medicaid is adopted, the States will now take over prime responsibility from the Federal Government for budgeting, controlling, and policing the Medicaid and Medicare systems. The States will be forced to find cost-saving measures, police frauds, and forgeries and dispense medical services within the available resources, etc. It is possible that the same current budget could be enough to provide more and better quality healthcare services.

(ix). Open up competition among healthcare providers.

Ideas such as public-run hospitals, clinics, and NGO health centers can be looked at by the States as a way of providing cheap or free Healthcare services to the less endowed sector of the general public. These services could help people who have no insurance. States can even encourage well-experienced doctors to use TV services and other satellite devices to provide expert knowledge which can help the people. There should also be a consideration for the people who have limited insurance who fall in the grey area because they have insurance that cannot cover some situations. All these people, plus others such as the visitors to the USA the undocumented residents, etc need medical services. In short, anybody not covered by insurance must be given alternatives including systems paid for through indirect taxation.

To illustrate this point of the grey area in healthcare I would like to mention the problems raised by the case of the Film John Q. Although not based on a true story, the circumstances are true to the present health care situation. The circumstances in the story could occur to anybody. In the story, John Q is acted by Denzel Washington as the lead character. He has a son who wanted to be a bodybuilder but developed a heart problem. The family was devastated. The insurance which they thought would assist them had altered their insurance terms by request from the employer and its value had dropped to a maximum of only US$ 20,000 dollars, the hospital told the family to raise US$ 250,000 dollars to cover the cost of the operation. The family sold all the assets they could sell and also received donations from friends and well-wishers but they could only raise another 22,500 dollars. The hospital could not help them and threatened to discharge his dying son.

Denzel Washington felt that he had to do something. He took over the ER section of the hospital and held people hostage until his case was resolved. During the ordeal, he came to learn from the hostages that insurance companies reward doctors and hospitals who do not take on complicated cases.

For fear of negative publicity, since the case had by now gone public, the hospital was forced to take on the case. Even if the employer had not altered the insurance provisions, the cost of the heart operation still could not have been covered by the insurance because the bill was too high. Such cases are common and can happen to anybody whether in low or middle-income groups.

Therefore the system should be structured in such a way that these scenarios can be covered by other alternatives such as public clinics and hospitals which can handle such cases without relying only on insurance coverage. These types of cases go on to mainly explain why 46% of bankruptcies are healthcare-related. Good people are pushed into this gray area out of no fault of their own and many times it drives them to end up in unnecessary financial difficulties which can cripple them for a long time.

In Uganda, where I was raised, 90% of the population is made up of peasants. The insurance system which had been put in place by the colonial masters collapsed because the peasants could not afford to pay the regular monthly installments on a regular basis. The country has therefore come to rely on a mixture of the government referral system covering from village clinics, sub country dispensaries, to district and national referral hospitals, church-owned clinics, and hospitals, plus privately owned clinics, dispensaries, and hospitals.

The government also financially supports private providers such as church-funded clinics and hospitals, clinics and hospitals run by

NGOs in order to provide affordable health services. In order to improve cash flows for the government hospitals, many of them provide a private paying wing for those who can afford to pay. Most of the district and national hospitals are semi-autonomous and self-accounting. This means that the income from the private wing does not go to the treasury but helps to improve health care services as government grants are usually insufficient to cover all the hospital expenses. The people are given all these options so that they can use the best options suited for their conditions. They have choices if they cannot afford the private clinics. They can go to a missionary hospital if they can raise some reasonable money. If they have no money at all they can use the free government facilities. Other developing countries such as Kenya, Ghana, and Tanzania have similar problems and solutions to their health care problems. Believe me, many people struggle to find ways not to use the less efficient free government medical facilities because they value their health. What is important is that despite little resources, the people have a choice.

Many people have suggested that in the case of the USA, either the system expands Medicaid to support the uninsured and other groups mentioned above or they should set up government or state-supported hospitals and clinics to cater for anybody who is not covered by the system. If the states or federal government do not want to run these institutions as a public entity, they can contract the private sector to run the service on their behalf through competitive bidding at as much a local level as possible. This would avoid creating big to fail monopolistic private corporations. This should also be able to ease the pressure on ER cases in the hospitals. These public hospitals, clinics, etc should be directly paid for by the federal government through the grant system to the states. The states can implement the system and the federal system can expand the block grants to also cover all the scenarios in the health care system. This would be a better alternative than the present system which forces people to buy insurance which they cannot afford. Forcing people to buy unaffordable services would lead to penalties and delinquencies which leave a bigger burden on the current health care insurance holders. It is like the housing bubble where people were sold houses that they could not afford to pay for and become toxic to the housing industry. Let people choose whatever health care service is best suited to them, provided there is open competition among all health care providers.

(x). Allow competition within the health care system;

Since the US believes in the competitive free market system, it should encourage other private, semi-private, nonprofit making organizations, businesses in public health services to live and compete alongside the existing health care systems. This should be encouraged to enable the free market system to provide services at the lowest best competitive cost. This would also provide alternate choices especially for those without health care insurance. The other good thing is that it will not put extra burden and cost on those using the health insurance system. In fact, this should reduce insurance premiums which presently put in a provision to cover patients treated without insurance coverage. The cost should be paid for directly by the federal governments through a transfer of funds to the states and to providers.

For instance, it is important to note that the education system encompasses the private, public, charter, and other types of schools which co-exist alongside one another. This allows people to choose the best system that they can afford. The system is working without much ado. Nobody is complaining that the public school system discourages other alternatives such as private schools. The same should happen to health care.

(xi). Adopt and implement good ideas from other countries

The USA should look at systems in other countries and adopt what is good. The aim should be to give universal health care services. With the present system, many people are still left out. The present public health system caters to the old age, disabled, and some of the low-income groups. About 18% of the population is still not included. These include the unemployed and under-employed.

We should also acknowledge the fact that there are as many as 12 million undocumented immigrants and there are also those whose immigration applications are still pending. There are also tourists and so many other people who come to the USA at any time for one reason or another. These are about 3 million at any one time. The health care system should cover all these situations.

(xii). Expand Funding of the Health care system

As mentioned before, most developed countries spend 10% of GDP to cover universal health care for their people. The US currently spends 16% of GDP but does not provide universal health care coverage. In order to bring the health care cost down the USA should also devise a system that provides choices. For instance, rich people may not need any insurance at all because they are able to pay for their health care needs through direct billing. The President, s Senators, Representatives. Judges, etc, because of the nature of their work may need a particular type of health care service. Spouses and children of the Presidents for security reasons may require a particular type of health care service. Busy people in public and private sectors may also require particular types of services to suit their busy schedules. Young people without complications may not need such comprehensive healthcare insurance until they become elderly. People who cannot afford health insurance may need government-supported healthcare services which should be paid for by public funds, donations, pro bono services, etc. The problem with Medicaid is that one has to qualify in order to be eligible for treatment. It is all based on income rather than need or choice. Health should be a service not based on social status.

(xiii) This burden of providing and paying for health care should be covered through taxation. At the moment part of the health care cost is covered by the working population through Medicare and disabled insurance contribution. It should however be noted that the ratio of FICA contributors has been on the decline partly because many companies have been adopting other cost-saving measures such as automation and overworking the workers to avoid employing more people. Employers who have adopted the automated systems don't have to contribute to FICA because they are no longer employing people. It is therefore logical that other types of taxation should be put in place to cover the health care needs of the people. The working people appear to be overburdened as one of the main contributors to the health care system. Therefore, I strongly recommend alternate revenue sources as follows:

(a) Introduction of a Medical Services Consumer Sales Tax;

The consumer sales tax for medical should be put in place to cater to the country's growing health care needs. It is believed that almost everybody will be happy to contribute to their well-being. This arrangement should not affect those who are getting their healthcare services through the insurance system as it is not designed to replace it. The system however would help those groups who do not have insurance for one reason or another and for those people with insurance which cannot cover all the unexpected circumstances. The system should also cover all other people residing in the USA at anytime since all will be contributing by paying the federal medical sales tax on goods and services. A visiting person in the USA who may need medical treatment will find it difficult to find a provider and the system is also expensive. If one requests for insurance cover, the insurance personnel will first ask for the social security number. Since the visitor does not have one, the insurance people will just hang up on them. Therefore , if all these groups pay for their sales tax medical fees imposed on goods and services, they will not be inconvenienced since they have already contributed and are covered through these indirect tax arrangements. The healthcare sales tax must only be used to provide healthcare services for everyone who needs treatment. This should include those who want to opt-out of FICA contributions .

(b) Increased Contributions from the richer people;

The other argument has been that the rich people should contribute a little more to cover government programs including healthcare. This is because it is thought that the rich are in a better position to contribute that little bit of extra than the lower-income counterparts. The following charts should give a better insight as to who is best suited to contribute more should there be a real need to increase taxation. Re: www.American.com/archive/2007/November-December-magazine-contents/guess.com. As can be observed by the charts 27% of the top-earning people pay 68% of the current government tax receipts. The top 50% pay 85% of the total tax revenue. The rest of the public contributes 13% of the total tax collection. On the other hand, we should consider that o the top 1% owns 42% of the financial wealth in the USA. The next 4% owns 27% of the wealth. The next 5% control another 11% of the financial wealth, the next 10% control 12% of the financial wealth. The rest of the population which is 80% owns about 10% of the country's financial wealth.

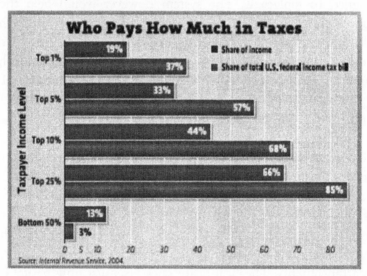

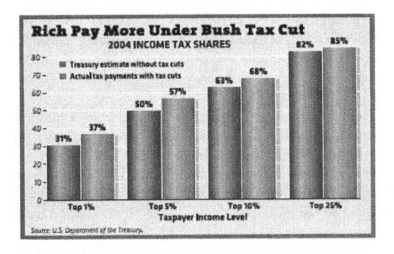

From the foregoing, it is clear who has the capacity to contribute more in form of taxes without much strain.

In good faith, the richer people should gladly be able to share a little bit more for any extra burden if it is required. This is in spite of the fact that they contribute a big percentage of government revenue. This is because 20% of the population owns 90% of the countries financial wealth. 80% of the population owns 10% of the countries wealth. It has also been observed that the 80% own a high percentage of credit card debt. The 80% are in a worse situation than the 20%. The only valid reason to request them to pay more is that they can better afford it. Before the government can increase taxes, it is very important to make an impact assessment on both the jobs and the economy so that the move is not counterproductive. There have been many cases where increases in taxes have negatively affected jobs and government revenue. We have to keep healthy the hen that lays the golden egg or the cow that produces milk. The one million dollar question is to get the balancing act right.

In conclusion, it can be argued that it is possible to provide healthcare for all people by providing healthcare competitive options that people can choose from to suit their individual needs. The cost of health care should come down to affordable levels through the free market competitive systems. USA can even provide cheaper and better quality health care service than the other OECD developed countries. However, the main aim is to provide health care for all. A HEALTHY NATION PRODUCES MAXIMUM RESULTS.

The healthcare tax is the way forward. Everyone contributes to their welfare. Those who want to have exclusive service can pay for themselves. The providers can be the private sector etc .since the government has not proved to be efficient. The collections must be separated from the General Fund and operated independently. This will remove politics out of healthcare. If they want insurance can help with operations at a fee, since they have the experience and networks they can compete at State or lower level for these services. I believe this can solve healthcare for good and for all.

CHAPTER 8

104) IMMIGRATION

(a) REMARKS

This is another one of the unsolved hot issues which should urgently be addressed and solved preferably on a nonpartisan basis. It is better than a committee looks at all issues surrounding immigration and recommend comprehensive solutions to congress for debate and adoption. The committee should be chaired by an independent but positive person and should include a wide range of as many participants as possible. Participation should include people from both sides of congress, the executive, different interested groups such as those who represent the people, immigration associations, churches, NGOs who deal with immigrant issues, lawyers, etc. Interested states, especially those who house legal and or illegal immigrants such as California, New Mexico, Arizona, Texas, etc should also be involved in these discussions. Representatives from affected countries such as Mexico, other Latino American countries, European, Asian, and African countries that have high immigrant populations in the USA should also be invited to attend either as observers or participants. This is because I believe that all these groups are part of the solution to the immigration problem. The idea is to find a genuinely comprehensive and humane solution to this difficult but manageable problem.

This is a very important issue because it involves the plight of about 12.5 million undocumented immigrants. The two USA political parties differ widely on solutions to the immigration issues

(b) REVIEW

The question of the immigration problem is not new. Between 1929 and 1939 USA forced over a million illegal Mexican and US citizens of Mexican origin to leave the country during the great depression. This was the time when Hubert Hoover was president of the United States. Hoover thought and believed that these immigrants were responsible for the adverse economic conditions which caused the depression. He believed that by sending away these aliens, both legal and illegal, the USA would solve the country's economic problem. Others thought that he had to find a scapegoat to blame for the country's economic woes and he calculated that the public would be pleased by the expulsion of the aliens.

In history, other countries have exercised similar cleansing policies. There have been expulsions and extermination of human beings which have been done in a harsh manner. Nobody will ever forget the sufferings of the Jews under Hitler. Recently there was the ethnic cleansing in the former Yugoslavia and it took the UNITED NATIONS, NATO, the USA, and other European countries to bring it to an end.

Another example of expulsions I can think of was in Uganda during the reign of H.E. Field Marshall President Iddi Amin Dada, VC, MC, and CBE. President Amin gave orders to the non-Ugandan Indians to leave the country within 90 days. Although Iddi Amin said that the expulsion order was as a result of a dream, some people believe that it was because one of the Indian ladies had rebuffed his advances. It is true that the Indian culture does not give freedom to Indian ladies to be free with other cultures and the women are scolded and punished if they dare to do so. However, constitutionally the lady was free to exercise her freedom of association and to stop or reject any unwanted advances even if this was from a whole president of the country.

The exodus caused a lot of chaos and protests from the Western world including the USA. The United Nations became involved and sent stateless Indians to countries such as Canada. A fund of US$ 40 million dollars was provided by the United Nations to handle the issue. The expulsion exercise involved only about 30,000 Indians mainly of British and Indian origin. However out of fear even some Ugandan citizens of Indian origin also panicked and left. Others who also left had Canadian, Indian, Pakistani citizenships but these were few. This exercise destabilized the British economy and their way of life there for some time. This was mainly because Indian culture makes it difficult for them to integrate with the western type of lifestyle. One can only imagine the chaos that would ensue if the US was to immediately expel the 12.5 million illegal immigrants.

Iddi Amin did not stop there. He went on and ordered the expulsion of nationals from other African countries such as Rwanda, Kenya, and Zaire claiming that these people were taking away jobs from Ugandan citizens jobs. What followed after the Rwandese nationals left is that there were no people left to attend to the sugarcane, tea, and tobacco plantations. This was because most of the sugarcane planters and cutters were mainly from Rwanda. Most of the Ugandans are mainly peasant farmers with their own homesteads and just enough land for their cash crops and food. They were therefore not interested in leaving their homesteads and move in to fill the gap left by the expelled sugarcane planters and cutters. As a result, the sugarcane plantations started growing into big wild bushes leading to declines in sugar and tea production. The Amin regime had miscalculated and the best they could do was to keep quiet and let the matter subside and wait for life to normalize.

Uganda which had been a net exporter of sugar had by then become a net importer of sugar. The sugarcane workers eventually returned to their jobs. Rwanda has little land and for them to export labor is a win-win situation with Uganda. This helps Uganda's economy to expand and in turn, Rwanda was provided with labor and jobs for their people. In any case, these immigrants spend much of the money in Uganda on such items as rent, food, education, etc. The actual net amount they send home is very negligible. Uganda and the neighboring countries therefore both gain economically.

This goes to show how poor decisions based on hate and short-sighted policies can be economically counterproductive for everybody concerned, in the short and long term. Today there is no animosity between Uganda and its neighbors. People move in and out of these countries without restrictions on their movements. The same thing could happen to the USA rather than have immigrants hiding in the USA for fear of not being able to move in and out freely without facing reprisals.

In Germany for instance, when Hitler had problems, he also blamed everything on the Jews. He did everything to punish them as a solution of dealing with the German problem. The Jews suffered greatly at the hands of the Gestapo and many perished under all sorts of conditions and circumstances. Many of the Jews perished in Gas Chambers.

(C) DEVELOPMENTS

(i). By 1964 however, the situation in the USA had changed. The 1964 Act reduced the immigration figures from 1 million to 165,000 per annum. However, all the neighboring countries such as Canada, Mexico, and other Latino American countries were exempted from this quota. They were treated as neighbors. In 1965, the quotas by country of origin were also abolished by the Hart-Cellar Act.

(ii). G.W.H Bush increased legal immigration by 40%. The commission set up by Bill Clinton however, recommended a reduction of legal immigration limits back to 550,000 per annum. Over this period between 1964 and 2000, over ten million people migrated to the USA but over half of those were illegal. By 2007 the population of illegal immigrants had grown to an estimated population of 12.5 million people.

(iii). The 2007 economic meltdown and the housing bubble have however brought back the matter of illegal immigration to center stage. A survey carried out regarding illegal immigration found that the number of people who would wish for stricter immigration laws and action had increased, but mainly for security reasons. This was mainly because this survey was carried out after the aftermath of the September 11 2001 attack on the USA. These numbers however vary greatly depending on which community is interviewed.(iv). During the 2008 election campaigns, immigration was one of the center stage political issues which were discussed and debated by various candidates at all levels.

(D) OBSERVATION

(i). One can therefore see that there is a distinct relationship between good and bad economic times with immigration policies pursued by the USA. Douglas Massey a Princeton sociologist who studies migration issues said the recession and lack of jobs are major factors in the decline of people entering the country illegally. President Ronald Reagan 1984, while debating Mondale in a televised campaign debate said, "I believe in the idea of amnesty for those who have put down roots and lived there, even though some time back they may have entered illegally". He was a sincere man with a vision and was not afraid for political reactions when stating what he thought was the right position on any issue.

It is important and interesting to note that many Republicans disagree with President Ronald Reagan's views on immigration issues. They are of the opinion his positions regarding immigration were misguided. In fact, to many Republicans, it is now taboo to even mention the word amnesty. Whoever mentions anything which could mean taking realistic and humane positions on immigration is attacked by the Republican leaderships at all levels. The pro conservative media networks are also part of this general negative attack against undocumented immigrants. Some political leaders and other people are afraid to say what they really feel about immigration issues and solutions there of due to possible reprisals from their fellow Republicans as this could lead to their political downfall.

The Republican leadership wants the public to perceive them as being tough on immigration matters. Free discussions on this issue are therefore no longer entertained by the pro-conservative organs and media. Some anti-immigration leaders are even being supported for being in support of and also practicing unconstitutional methods of dealing with immigration issues. They are being praised especially by the pro-conservative media for saying that the federal government has failed to act, relentlessly and possibly ruthlessly in implementing immigration laws. Some media commentators even go as far as encouraging States to take immigration implementation into their own hands, although they at the same time say it is a federal responsibility. There are some political leaders who are even advocating that children of illegal immigrants should be denied citizenship and should be deported. They even advocate that those people who received citizenship but fall into the above category should also have their citizenship revoked. They, however, do not mention the cut-off date for these cancellations. Maybe to be fair they should recommend that we should go back as far as those who first landed on the American continent and found the original Red Native American Indians who are now living in the native reservations.

(ii). To be realistic and legalistic them Red Indians should be the ones to decide on visa issues for all immigrants who have displaced them. Even in some less developed countries, anyone born in that country's air space has a right to claim citizenship if he or she wishes to do so. Some countries even allow for dual citizenship. America is known to be a land of immigrants and therefore should be more tolerant and understandings as far as immigration issues are concerned. Many people are here because of the American dream and that is what makes American what it is today. In fact, the demographics of the American population have changed tremendously over the last 100 years, and there is no way of reverting back to the old population percentages.

Many people, especially the conservatives, are shouting for the building of a fence along the USA Mexican border and strictly enforce the existing laws without any further reviews or delays. If this view of strict enforcement of the immigration laws is strictly imposed, this would mean immediate expulsion of the 12.5 million illegal immigrants no matter what their individual circumstances are. This would be the biggest exodus since the Jews left Egypt or ten times the expulsion numbers during the 1933 to '39 exodus ordered by Edgar Hoover. Such a move could bring untold catastrophic consequences and suffering for both the USA and the other countries involved.

(iii). The economic impact on the USA losing 12.5 million consumers would also affect the country in many ways. The present housing bubble could in fact explode beyond the current level since the landlords would start struggling to find new tenants to replace those who have left. Retail department stores would also find it hard to fill a vacuum of those people who have left. That is why it would be better to use a less violent and humane solution to the immigration problem. The best way would mean involving all stakeholders to come to the table and hammer out a long-term immigration solution.

(E) PAST LEGISLATION

(i). Congress has tried to find a solution to immigration over the years but lacks the political will to act because of the seemingly irreconcilable political differences between the two parties. If one side supports and suggests one solution the other side must oppose the measure and for most likely political reasons other than the essence of the proposed measure. In 2006 for instance, the House of Representatives passed the border protection and anti-terrorism and illegal immigration act of 2005. The Senate on the other hand passed the immigration reform act of 2006. But as everyone expected everything fell apart at the conference stage as both versions failed to be reconciled because partly the house version was more radical and but mainly due to the fact that no side was willing to give in. Furthermore, many members from both houses who were opposed to the immigration reform bill were spitting venom and had vowed to kill the bill during the conference stage. Indeed the bill lapsed during the conference stage as had been expected.

(ii). President Bush had supported the 2006 senate bi-partisan effort which had been proposed by the Republican Senator McCain and the late democratic senator Teddy Kennedy for the Senate version of the bill. These senate measures would have involved the setting up of a guest worker program and would also include a path to citizenship. The measure would also have supported securing a partial border fence to be built along the US/Mexican Border. The measure would further have in the meantime encouraged the enforcement of the present laws.

(F) OTHER PAST MEASURES

(i). Earlier in 1986, the Reagan administration also had taken steps to solve the immigration problem. President Ronald Reagan signed the 1986 immigration reform and coastal Act. The aim of the measure would be to eradicate illegal immigration. The act called for the following:

a) Strict penalties for employers who hire undocumented workers.

b) Amnesty for illegal immigrants who entered the country before 1982. 2.9 million Illegal immigrants out of an estimated 3.2 million positively responded to the amnesty.

There was however nothing concrete put in place to strictly enforce the new provisions of the Act. This is partly why we are still faced with the same problem today. Another problem was that there was nothing put in place for those people who had entered the USA illegally between 1982 and 1986 when the amnesty act was enacted.

Ronald Reagan was very passionate about issues regarding immigration including illegal immigration. For example, in 1979 while having a private meeting with President Jose Lopez Portillo of Mexico, Reagan is said to have expressed the wish that they could make the border discussion on something other than the location of a fence. When Ronald Reagan met with the Soviet leader, then Secretary-General Mikhail Gorbachev, Reagan challenged him to tear down the Berlin wall. This was during a speech commemorating the 750th anniversary of Berlin. Reagan reasoned that the move would advance the cause for world peace and advance human liberty. The wall which was a symbol of the iron curtain was meant to seal the East Germany communist control zone from contact with the Free democratic West Berlin and West Germany and the capitalist world. Those people in East Germany, East Berlin who wished to cross to W. Berlin were not allowed to do so by the Soviet Union and East German authorities. There was no freedom of speech, movement, and other basic human rights in the East communist-controlled parts of Germany. The Soviet Union controlled its union and the satellite states with an iron hand.

Against all these odds, many East German people made daring moves to cross to West Germany mainly through crossing the Berlin Wall. They used all sorts of methods such as driving cars, trucks, etc through the barricades built by Soviet and East German authorities. Other methods used to cross included underground tunnels, sewerage systems just to mention but a few. Some made it but many perished at the hands of the German and Russian authorities while trying to gain their freedom.

There was great jubilation in 1989 when the Berlin wall was allowed to be brought down. This was followed a few years later with the beginning of the meltdown of the cold war. Thanks to Mikhail Gorbachev and Ronald Reagan, Germany is now one strong united country and most of Eastern Europe is now free.

(ii). Reagan's approach to immigration was the exact opposite of Hubert Hoover who kicked out 1 million illegal and legal immigrants and forced them to be sent back to their countries of origin. That is the difference in approach by these two leaders of the same country.

(G) Observations On Mexico Immigration Issues

(i). Mexico is responsible for 60% of the illegal immigrants in the USA. The other Latin American states are responsible for another 20%, Asia is 12%, Europe, and Africa is 8%. Mexico and the other Latin American states make up about 80% of the illegal American population in America. The solution to immigration must therefore take these percentages in mind.   On the other hand, Mexico also has immigrants' problems from the neighboring countries such as Guatemala, Honduras, El Salvador, Cuba, Ecuador, but also as far as China, S. Africa, and Pakistan. The Mexican government deports or repatriates some of their immigrants every year. However, Mexico at the same time is known to be encouraging its citizens to migrate to the USA because it is said that they give information and advice to Mexican citizens on how to immigrate to the USA. They force people to leave Mexico but at the same time, they encourage their people to migrate to the USA.

According to many sources, Mexico has a population of about 110 million people with a per capita income of approximately US $15,323. In 2009 Mexico was classified as a high-income country. Mexico has a steady annual economic growth rate of 7.6%. It is considered an industrialized country. It is 11th in the world by purchasing power. It is 10th in the world as a tourist center. It has a US $55 billion trade surplus with the USA. It is a free mixed economy. Mexico has a vibrant economy and did not get affected so badly during the 2007 economic and housing breakdown. Therefore there are absolutely not so many good reasons why so many of its citizens should be suffering illegally here in the USA. Surely there is an obligation by the Mexican government to find ways to offload some of the illegal immigrant burdens on the USA. Mexico's economy is growing faster than that of the USA. That is why I am of the opinion that they should be part of the solution by taking part in the proposed immigration solutions committee, or another discussion.

(ii). Apart from the immigration problem, Mexico has other multiple problems to solve with the USA. These include the drug curtails, the fighting along the common US-Mexican border on the Mexican side, high crimes along the border, and also crimes committed inside the USA. These other crimes include murder and rape within the USA perpetrated mainly by the criminal and drug gangs. The other Latin states also have similar problems save for the Mexican severe drug gang problem. All these problems need a concerted effort to find solutions by all of those involved or affected.

(H) GENERAL POSSIBLE ACTIONABLE ANSWERS TO IMMIGRATION

While trying to solve the immigration problem there are some solutions that can be looked at and if they are found to be reasonable, they could be adopted and implemented and within a reasonable period, the immigration problem could be a thing of the past.

(i). First, locate and identify the people The first thing the USA should do is locate and identify who these illegal immigrants are. This can be done by issuing all illegal immigrants with mandatory interstate passes. These passes can be used by the immigrants to move in and out of the USA while a possible permanent solution to the immigration problem is being worked out. This is because most of these illegal immigrants have roots here which they cannot abandon overnight. Of course, they should pay for these interstate passes maybe something like $50 to $100 renewable every three years. This could generate $1.25 billion for the treasury over the three years. Once every person now has an identification document, then it will first of all be easier to isolate the wrongdoers and deal with them decisively. At the end of the exercise, anybody who does not have this document can either voluntarily leave the country immediately or be deported for lack of identification. Simple deportation measures can be instituted to quicken the process. No employer will be advised to employ anybody without these interstate passes.

(ii). In the case of the USA neighbors such as Mexico, it is first of all important to realize that both these peoples have been crisscrossing the borders for centuries as a result of these contacts many people from both sides have intermarried and have already changed the demographics of the US population. The USA has also many people with roots from Europe who came as Settlers. The USA also has over one million of its citizens settled in Mexico.

(iii). The effect of the proposed interstate passes is that it will free the people and will result in increased inter border crossing. Once people are free to move in and out without fear , the number of illegal immigrants will decrease because people will know that they are not going to be denied re-entry once they move out of USA.

Instead of moving families to the USA, only essential people will be migrating to the USA to find jobs and they will stay only for short periods at a time because they will go to see their families then return. The same concept happens in South Africa where many people from other countries provide work as coal and diamond diggers etc to South Africa. These concepts are not only unique to the USA. I understand the same concept is practiced in Canada.

(iv). The USA can also issue specific social security numbers for people with interstate passes which can allow people to access other services until all other matters are regularized. Social security numbers have been integrated in the USA for many systems and services.

(v). The other advantage is that once everybody has a document it will be easier to locate and deal with drug dealers and addicts, gang members, and other serious crime offenders. It will also be easy to know the magnitude of the problem. This will also assist in knowing who comes in and out.

(vi). As regards the insecurity, crime, and drug problems along the US-Mexican border, the USA must get involved because they are the main target since the drugs are targeted for the USA market. These drug lords are reckoned to have a network of over 100,000 employees many of whom are armed and can be dangerous and deadly. Some sources put the figure of the network at over one million people.

The border area between Mexico and the USA, therefore, needs special attention. The drug wars have turned the Mexican side of the border into another Wild Wild West. In those days at least they had men of true grit as depicted in the western films which portray actors such as John Wayne, Yul Brynner, Steve McQueen, Billy the Kid, etc, men who could face these criminals and eliminate them for the good of humanity. We do not have such men anymore. We instead we have gangs and pirates such as those in Somalia who even have the leverage to get ransom from legitimate governments. They seem to terrorize the population without many confrontations. The USA should not stand by as a neighbor and keep blaming Mexico for all these atrocities. The USA has troops in Iraq, Afghanistan, Korea and so many other places where they have intervened in order to stabilize these areas. It is therefore strange that they make Mexico an exception, especially when most of the drugs are sold in the USA, and all these incidents of shootings and murder can spill over or affect events in the USA.

Immediate international action is, therefore, necessary to bring sanity to these areas. If the Red brigades were defeated, so should the Mexican border drug warlords. The USA with the neighboring countries and or the United Nations should join Mexico in a once and for all effort to fix these outlaws. We should not just sing and press for building the border fence to lock out these Mexicans. We should help our neighbors Mexico etc get rid of the problem. Like how fire spreads without regard to borders so will the insecurity caused by these gangs at the Mexico/ USA border area. It is regrettable that the United Nations is no longer as strong as before. Countries now use the UNO whenever it is convenient and not whenever it is necessary. Gone are those days of action during when there were Secretary Generals" such as Butrus Butrus Ghali etc.

(vii). It is important to also note that these drug dealers have to clean their $40 billion annual sales in the USA into usable funds. It is generally understood that they are cleaning their money and channeling the money mainly using USA banks. More strict measures possibly through a permanent task force doing nothing else but tracing these transfers should be put in place. If effectively enforced, this measure alone might break the back of this dangerous business

The USA and Mexico should also liaise with suppliers of all sorts of other types of drugs such as ecstasy from China, cocaine from Columbia and other Latin-American countries as a way to reduce the supply routes and availability of these equally dangerous drug alternatives.

(H) OTHER OBSERVATIONS AND SOLUTIONS;

What is important to note is that many people have become illegal as a result of unrealistic USA policies and punitive laws currently in force. These policies include the following points:—

(a) It takes too many years to review one's case if that person was deported because of visa issues. This is especially painful if one has family ties in the USA. This is one of the main reasons why many people stay put once they are in the country. Relax the law then it will look as if one has opened the prison gates of political prisoners. People will come out of hiding

(b) It takes months to get a US visa appointment in some countries. On top of that, every time applicants who go for interviews have to pay as much as $200 per visit. Imagine countries with a per capita income of less than US$1000. Two visits to the embassy and 50% of the applicants' annual income is swallowed by visa fees. Is that not punitive on the side of the USA to charge US rates to third world countries whose per capita income is much lower than that of the USA, and whose salaries are much lower than that of the USA? The exercise is misunderstood by many people as being commercial other than the original intention.

(c) The attitude of many of the embassy officials conducting the interviews requires a lot of reviews. The USA should get people trained as diplomats with mannerisms and eliquate associated with diplomatic services. The negative attitude makes many people including V.I.P,s fear that next time their applications may be denied.

(d) The percentage of successful applicants for visa interviews is reckoned to be less than 10% of the applicants. Visa quotas should be increased for other people other than the U.S.A. neighboring countries. Genuine applications for people who want to take up opportunities in the USA should be looked at more favorably. Most important people should be treated with dignity.

(e) I hope that what has been suggested gives some input in finding solutions to immigration and other related problems. It is important to make this perceived, immigration problem a thing of the past. We love the USA as the vanguard of democracy and we should find ways for the USA to make it stronger for the good of world peace and human development.

CONCLUSION

In the USA it is observed by the CATO institute that each illegal immigrant family in the USA contributes about 80,000 US dollars to the US economy, on average, during the time they stay in the country. This is contrary to the belief held by many people especially the conservative group, that these illegal immigrants are parasitic on the US economy. Maybe a joint study over the issue could dig out the truth and come up with the real facts. This will help people to make decisions based on properly researched accurate information.

When people know from an informed angle regarding the facts about immigration, maybe once all these facts will help people get humane and fair decisions. This will lead to a lasting solution and end unnecessary animosity.

CHAPTER 9

105) ENERGY ISSUES AND SOLUTIONS

Energy is one of the controversial and yet essential issues that Congress must attend to and address because it affects the economy in many ways. It is important that energy issues should be addressed in a comprehensive manner rather than using a piecemeal and selective approach.

105A) ENERGY SOURCES

(i) General Remarks.

The USA gets its energy from many sources. In 2007 the following sectors and percentages of energy sources were recorded. (See. http:www.en.wikipedia.org/wiki/Energy_policy_of_the_United_States).

    a) Petroleum 37.1%
    b) Coal 22.5%
    c) Natural gas 23.8%
    d) Nuclear 8.5%
    e) Renewable energy (mainly from hydro-electric dams, wind, geo-thermo and solar 7.3%)

105B) ENERGY CONSUMPTION

(ii) General remarks

In the same year, USA consumed its energy by sector was as follows:

a) Transport 29%

b) Industrial 21%

c) Residential and Commercial 10%

d) Electrical 40%

105C) Energy Policy

The USA consumes 21 million barrels of oil per day and out of this 6 million is procured locally. At an average of 100 dollars per barrel, the USA pays about 547 billion dollars a year in oil imports.

It is however important to note that the USA has enough coal and natural gas reserves to serve our energy needs for the next 100 years. The USA is also known to have massive oil reserves embedded in oil sands.

Despite all this good news it is unfortunate to note that the USA does not have a comprehensive energy plan to eventually meet the country's present and future energy needs.

Some policy mandates have been made over the years and three energy policy acts have been passed in congress in the years 1992, 2005, and 2007. Many of the provisions passed include energy conservations, energy development, grants, and tax incentives for all sorts of energy initiatives. The current Obama administration has proposed energy reforms which include a reduction in carbon dioxide emissions with a cap and trade tax program with an emphasis on providing and developing clean renewable sustained energy, initiatives.

However, none of the above plans or policies provides comprehensive short or long-term plans that will gradually make USA energy sufficient in the long term. The reasons for having this policy are vital for both economic and security reasons. It is vital for the USA to put in place a long-term program that examines all the available energy sources and provides a long-term plan to supply the people with the cheapest and environmentally friendly energy as soon as possible. The long-term plan should also provide for and encourage other unknown new energy sources which might develop along the way. These issues are vital and must therefore be addressed without further delay by congress because energy affects a whole range of economic activities. Energy as already mentioned forms a vital part of the long-term economic and security strategic planning for the USA.

Among other considerations, the energy plan should include the following points.

(a) Itemize all the current energy sources

(b) Put in place research plans for the present and future energy sources for all possible energy sources.

(c) Encourage competition in the energy sector for present and future sources. Such a policy will ensure that current sources with comparative advantages are encouraged and harnessed to provide the people with the cheapest available energy alternatives.

If the above policies are put in place, resultant benefits will include the following:—

(i) Job opportunities will be created as those happening in North Dakota.

(ii) The economy will be stimulated and expanded.

(iii) The chances of energy blackmail by other major energy product producers will be minimized.

(iv) The competition created will ensure cheap energy for the people.

(v) Other sectors of the economy will be positively affected by cheap energy prices and this will make the country benefit and experience economic growth in almost all sectors.

(vi) The USA will ensure comparative advantages over other countries and USA products will be able to find overseas markets.

From the foregoing, it is rather important for the Administration and Congress to urgently find a nonpartisan energy solution to give the people energy at the cheapest possible cost. Power and transport affect prices on a whole range of products through the whole economy. Partisan interests and bickering must fall by the wayside, and a pro-America solution must be found and implemented sooner rather than later. Delaying glaring opportunities for possible economic growth must not be entertained since such opportunities must be encouraged to maintaining the USA's economic superiority over the other countries.

During the 2008 election campaigns, when the gas price hit $3 per gallon, the Democrats made a lot of capital out of this. They accused Bush and his Vice of purportedly having vested interests in the oil business. They wanted Congress to impose a surtax on excess profits by oil businesses. When the gas price went over $4 a gallon even most of the rest of the population rightly started thinking that there was definitely something wrong and that the Democrats could have had a cause to complain in the first place. This issue must have cost the Republicans many votes during the 2008 elections.

The Administration, Congress, and oil companies did not pinpoint and tell the public what was causing these price hikes. Some economists claimed that the price hikes were caused by speculative interests. They also blamed refineries for deliberately producing under capacity so that they could rip excessive profits. Oil companies were definitely making record profits. The sudden hike in gas prices resulted in higher prices in a wide range of goods and services. High prices were also almost crippling the trucking business itself. Sales of SUVs started dropping rapidly in favor of smaller gas-saving vehicles. The general state of the economy had started causing concern.

Suddenly to everybody's surprise, the price of oil started dropping from almost $150 per barrel to around $48 per barrel over a very short period. The Administration, Congress, or oil companies did not explain this sudden turn of events. Companies that were involved in this oil price speculation were suddenly heading for bankruptcy. Eventually, the price settled for some time between $60 and $70 a barrel. Prices stabilized and the economy started recovering. Congress which had promised to investigate these speculative actions seems to have come to no conclusive explanation and the issue seems to have been forgotten.

One possible answer is that companies wishing to buy oil in futures and did not end-users had to deposit a higher margin for the amounts committed to ordering. This is one of the main weapons that was used to bring the oil prices down. I do not see why the measure cannot be used as a weapon to minimize speculative tendencies in the oil procurement business. There are accusations being made that some of the high-ranking officers in the present administration, particularly those working in the energy sector hold the view that oil prices should be allowed to rise high enough to allow other energy alternatives to be able to compete favorably. They were trying to promote renewable energy sources and this did not look good for the economy.

If this is true it is sad because this would discourage the extension of the economy and undermine the advantages the USA is enjoying to produce cheaper goods for both domestic and export markets. Another way that can be used to reduce procurement costs is to encourage bilateral arrangements with oil-producing countries and obtain oil at either discounted prices or fixed prices for a specific period. The latter was used by southwest airlines to secure guaranteed cheaper aviation fuel.

I remember when I was the vice-chairman Eastern of Uganda National Chamber of Commerce, we received a delegation from one of the Middle East countries. This was under the Chairmanship of AL Haji Sulaiman Masaaba.

The delegation was prepared to give Uganda 30% discount on current oil prices at the time provided the country procured all the oil requirements from them.

When I introduced the idea to the concerned government executives, they were not interested even to discuss the issue with the delegation citing current procurement arrangements through the oil companies.

This however goes to show that where there is a will there is a way because these oil-producing countries are also looking for a higher share of the market. They can therefore discount their prices.

The move by South West Airlines to negotiate long-term aviation energy delivery arrangements was a smart idea. The airline is making profits and they are not loading customers with extra expenses such as baggage fees like what the other limping airlines are doing. Yes, it is possible to keep gas prices down and reasonable to the consumer with correct policies and decisions.

As of now, oil prices have again shot up. A barrel of oil is hovering between $90 and $110. The gas prices have now settled over $3 a gallon and nobody is screaming like they did when Bush was in power. Congress and the administration are quiet and so are the left-leaning media networks which used to make noise about rising oil prices. Some left-leaning people are said to be recommending that gas prices should be hiked to be in line with European gas price levels. They are said to argue that this would reduce demand and also make it profitable to develop go green energy renewable alternatives. This kind of thinking appears to be dangerous and counterproductive to economic recovery and development.

(105D)CURRENT ENERGY POLICY

There is reason and concern to believe that the main thrust of the current administration's energy policy is towards the development of clean green energy. The idea of clean green energy is good but what the USA and or the world needs is cheap affordable energy. Right now there is a deliberate emphasis on solar, wind, and other renewable energy sources. The administration also seriously wants to address global warming by imposing a carbon tax but this will also mean a high price to the ordinary consumer. The new carbon tax would increase energy costs an extra US$2,000 a year for the average family. This would appear unpopular since most people at this juncture badly need cheaper energy because of the current global recession.

The Administration was bent on going green no matter what the cost of energy production and the cost to the taxpayer. The consumer is likely to face higher prices to cover the extra production costs.

On top of all this, the administration is also seriously in support of the carbon tax and global warming initiatives. The global warming initiatives hit a highlight in Copenhagen. During the conference in Copenhagen, the US and Europe tried to sell the idea of the carbon tax to the rest of the world. They even proposed and supported aUS$100 billion dollars to support the poor and developing countries who would suffer as a result of these measures. The US administration and top leaders from congress on both sides of the parties all converged in Copenhagen to put their case. The President's team and the Democrats in Congress were supporting the measure while the Republicans in Congress were de-campaigning the carbon tax measures. Eventually, the whole exercise was watered down because countries like China and India who would suffer most from these measures did not wholly support the proposal.

There is nothing wrong with all these moves provided they are based on proven scientific data and conclusions. On the contrary, what is happening is that whoever has any differing views or data that person is immediately attacked by the global warming vested interests. This is despite the fact that scientists who produced the present policies on global warming admitted having relied on doctored data. It is not right for the world to still stick and rely on questionable conclusions from distorted data.

People should not be forced or enticed into putting billions of peoples' Tax dollars in questionable ventures. What is worse is that the world bodies and countries with vested interests are forcing the world to go along with the present policies. It seems all they are interested in, is to make quick bucks.

The only way forward is to review all the possible theories and come out with the correct positions or decisions. The United Nations should invite all the scientists and open up discussion on what to do with the perceived theory of global warming.

It is important that anybody with data and ideas should be listened to. After all nobody has a monopoly of what Mother Nature can do and therefore it is important to listen to everybody with an idea instead of trashing those ideas before they are listened to.

We can all see the earthquake that hit Japan recently and what happened to the nuclear reactors. Nobody was expecting the damage that was caused and no clear explanations have been advanced.

We should not as owners of mother earth move on with unproven and questionable directions, and invest vast resources that may be tomorrow's embarrassment. People must know what is involved and they must not be enticed in taking a leap in the dark.

At the time when we are having a recession, it is not logical to initiate expensive energy measures when people are instead looking forward to even cheaper energy prices. The best policy is for Congress and the administration to support all efforts being made to produce cheap and clean energy as soon as possible. This does not mean that environmental concerns should not be weighed in but it should not be the only factor that determines the choice of the present and future energy sources. The first and most paramount factor should be affordable energy at the cheapest possible cost. This will at least ensure sustained economic development.

(105E) THE FUTURE OF ENERGY IN USA

What is important is for Congress and the Administration to support all current and future energy initiatives and give all current and future ideas equal support. We should not favor one source of energy sources over another. In the 2012 budget proposal for instance, the administration is proposing to spend 3.7 billion dollars for green energy initiatives. This is probably on top of the US$60 billion originally approved in the stimulus act, although it is said that the above figure of US$ 60 billion was later scaled down a bit. While this is good, this money should be used to assist research in any existing and new energy initiatives so that there is equal opportunity for all energy sector initiatives. Current provable sources must also be financed so that cheaper energy ideas are developed. The Administration must avoid choosing winners and losers because this is dangerous to the US economy. It would not be prudent to support only one sector which might even turn out to be a red herring. We would have backed on the wrong horse at a high financial cost and a gross loss of time. Congress should be tough with the Administration and approve the use of these funds to fund research in all the energy sectors.

Congress should also look and assess the impact on the economy for those programs already approved and see whether they are economically viable investments likely to produce positive results for the US economy and environment.

The following are some of the programs which are receiving subsidies from the government. Programs that are negatively impacting the economy should be treated as research items other than business investment programs because in many ways they distort the concept of the free market system. The economy will most likely suffer as a result of higher prices for the consumers just to benefit a few clever people who can manipulate the system to the detriment of the rest of the population for their benefit.

a) Chevy electric car:

The Chevy electric car is being subsidized by government support to the extent of US$7,500 per unit. There are arguments that if many people buy electric cars because of the above subsidy, such cars are going to use electricity for recharging the batteries, and yet this power is generated from coal. This could be counterproductive especially since there already is a move to discourage coal production. This could end up in higher energy prices. Instead of subsidies, Congress can fund further research in the project of what appears to be a promising energy alternative. It might be wiser to also encourage more production of other known alternatives such as natural gas. Competition is the key and further research might help electric car manufacturers to produce less expensive models which can economically compete with the current vehicle models without dependency on subsidies. Until that is possible, it makes economic sense to treat this program purely as a research item and not as an immediate alternative to the current economically cheaper energy-consuming vehicles. The research project can produce a few vehicles for testing purposes until their running costs and safety standards are in line with current regulations.

b) Ethanol At the moment Congress is subsidizing corn growers to encourage them to produce enough raw materials for securing the required ethanol production percentages. This measure is as a result said to increase gas prices because of the high cost of producing ethanol. At this time when prices of gas are so high, many people question whether it is prudent to spend taxpayers' money to produce uneconomically viable products such as ethanol. Subsidizing ethanol has also other multiplier effects.

(i) It increases the prices of other products such as milk, meat, etc which use corn as a raw material. Many people now cannot afford to buy as much milk and meat as they used to because of these new high prices.

(ii) Another multiplier effect is that as a result of higher gas prices partly because of the high ethanol subsidies and production costs, transport costs have generally increased and this, in turn, has also meant higher prices of other commodities across the board. This is because transporters have to charge higher prices to cover the increase in fuel prices.

(iii) Ethanol also has another problem such as the transport of its raw materials for refining and blending. Ethanol can only be transported to the refineries by trucks because of its characteristics whereas petroleum can be transported by other means including the use of pipelines.

(iv) Ethanol is also more costly to process. According to some economists, it should be a net loser because to them it costs more to produce ethanol per gallon than the price it is being sold at. Ethanol is less efficient than oil. It is estimated after all these costs are put together it costs approximately 50 cents more per gallon to produce ethanol than the present oil sources. This, therefore, makes the pump price to be more expensive as the ethanol loss has to be passed on to the end-user.

(v) So far US$35 billion has been spent on ethanol subsidies. Many people question whether the economy can continue to sustain such subsidies for long periods without causing unnecessary economic consequences. This is definitely an unnecessary burden to the taxpayer. It would be more prudent to invest the money in research and production of other cheaper sources such as natural gas. Natural gas is abundant and emits 60% lower emissions compared to coal and would produce cheaper energy in the immediate and foreseeable future. Other sources such as algae fuel which have a good promising future should also receive equal treatment as renewable fuels. At this time we cannot afford to pick winners and losers. No one knows when the next cheap energy source will spring from. We must finance research programs for all possibilities.

(105F). Recently, the House passed the Waxman-Markey cap and trade bill which would have forced each family to annually spend about an extra US$2000 dollars in energy costs. The house passed the 1,428-page bill without much debate and without most representatives having read and understood its implications just like they did with the health care act. The bill, fortunately, did not pass through the Senate despite efforts by the administration to have it bulldozed through Congress before the November 2010 midterm elections. According to the Heritage Foundation, the bill could also cost the country about 2 million jobs. As an example, it is said that the 2006 California assembly bill No. 32 led to higher energy costs and job losses in California. It is reasoned that in Spain, for every one job gain as a result of cap and trade, the economy loses 2.2 other jobs. It is therefore said that this is a net job loser and should be discouraged. All these examples go on to support the view that we should not pre-determine the energy sources of the future.

The ordinary consumer is left with the burden of the increased prices of products and services across the board.

(105G) CURRENT CHEAPER OIL ENERGY SOURCES

Below are some of the other cheaper energy sources.

(a) Offshore Drilling   The current policy for offshore drilling is puzzling. Although the Administration lifted the ban on offshore drilling after the BP fiasco, it appears no new licenses have been issued. The spirit of "drill baby drill" for oil seems to be negatively perceived by the Administration. The Administration should be encouraging every possible opportunity towards the goal of getting the USA to achieve cheap energy independence. This is very important especially taking into account of what is happening in the Middle East. We should not forget what Saddam Hussein did in Kuwait just before and during Desert Storm. While Iraqi troops were fleeing Kuwait they burnt as many oil wells as they possibly could and it took time to make them operational. The Libyan leader was also threatening to do the same if the demonstrators did not stop their rebellion. The question of energy independence now supersedes such considerations as to first go green and then consider energy independent later.

(b) Natural gas Companies, people, institutions, etc dealing in natural gas initiatives have been complaining that they do not get enough attention and support from the administration. Cars and trucks using natural gas perform well but there is a need to give the sector more in form of further research to address the remaining teething problems.

One of the main drawbacks of natural gas as fuel for vehicles is the gas tanks for storing liquid gas. Gas tanks occupy a lot of space and therefore they leave very little trunk space. This problem can be solved or improved upon once enough resources for further research are provided. The other drawback is that there are very few natural gas filling stations which I am sure can also be resolved very quickly. The natural gas and the oil companies which already have gas station networks can collaborate to find solutions to some of these issues.

(c) Oil sands reserve   It is reckoned that world oil sand reserves have as much oil potential as the oil reserves of Saudi Arabia. Oil sand deposits are mainly found in Canada and Venezuela which own reserves of about 1.25 trillion barrels each. The USA has moderate oil sand deposits of about 32 billion barrels of oil.

Canada produces 40% of its oil production from oil sands. This means that it is also a viable source of energy for USA deposits despite small differences in methods to be used to harness this abundant resource.

There are reports that new technology has been developed to make the recovery of the oil sands commercially viable and environmentally friendly. Despite all this, it is believed that environmentalists and the EPA are planning to frustrate these initiatives, especially with very stringent administrative regulations.

For the foreseeable future, it is only logical to exploit the known reserves because they are economically advantageous. This will help especially the USA to further grow its economy and in this way, the country can be able to stabilize the national debt and at the same time be able to finance research in future energy alternatives. It is illogical at the moment to only pursue the very expensive energy sources at the expense of the known cheaper sources. Such initiatives are not yet commercially viable and therefore should still be treated as research programs.

(d) Oil shale reserves (see.www/cn.wikipedia.org/wiki/oil_shale)

Oil shale resources are found mainly in 33 countries. Those deposits are of commercial value with current technology but the figures can increase as technology improves. A 2005 estimate sets oil shale deposits at 411 gigatons enough to yield 2.8 to 3.3 trillion barrels of oil. This compares favorably to world-proven oil reserves at 1.317 trillion barrels. 62% of these oil shale resources occur in the United States mainly in the green River formation which covers portions of Colorado, Utah, and Wyoming. 70% of this land is government-owned.

The above world figures do not appear to include deposits found in China which could increase the estimate of recoverable reserves. There are challenges to the extraction of oil from this source and most methods are still in the experimental stage. Only four methods appear to have been successfully tested and remain in commercial use.

In order to make it commercially viable, the price of crude oil must be above the US$70 to US$95 range per barrel of crude oil. There are suggestions that the costs for extraction of this resource could be brought down to US$30 to US$40 per barrel after the extraction of the first one billion barrels of oil just as prices always fall after investors have recovered their investment costs.

Availability of water in the arid sections of the Green River area also poses technical problems. There are also other environmental challenges to be considered and reduce to tolerable levels. These include acid drainage, oxidation of buried materials, contamination of surface water by materials such as mercury, possible changes in the ecosystems in the mining areas, carbon dioxide, and greenhouse gases. Section 526 of the Energy Independence and Security Act Prohibits USA agencies from buying oil produced by processes that produce more greenhouse gas emissions than would traditional petroleum methods. More research is therefore needed to quell the fears of Environmentalists and the EPA which also appears to be antagonistic to the idea of harnessing this source of oil shale deposits.

The USA government should spend more resources in research efforts in order to harness this God-given abundant resource.

(e). Expand drilling from already known reserves. The administration should give more licenses to companies so that there is an expansion of oil production from the currently known reserves. There are many people who claim that the administration is not entirely encouraging the idea by playing delaying tactics. They take too long to grant the licenses. Since the BP fiasco, they are taking the time to lift the suspension and speedily grant oil drilling permits in a timely manner especially those from government-owned lands. The government should behave as if there is urgency in giving local production the prominence it deserves, by opening up more oil wells from known current oil reserves. It is amazing to see how the oil business in North and South Dakota has brought dramatic economic changes to these two states with very little government support. These two states need government assistance in providing infrastructure, housing, etc so that all these other services can develop in line with the oil boom taking place in these two states. North Dakota had the lowest unemployment rate according to the Nov 2011 unemployment report. This is in contrast with the go green initiatives. Go green projects they say are not producing the same impact despite the enormous amount of money which has been injected. Many people are wondering why the government is reluctant to encouraging such viable current solutions which are attracting so many jobs and expanding the economy. What we are doing is like telling Saudi Arabia to discourage oil production and go green. This is because green clean energy might be one of the energy sources in the next century or beyond, but not for now.

In conclusion, every initiative current and future must be encouraged and supported without any reservations because you never know where the answer to cheap energy will emanate from. These current known alternate sources will guarantee cheap energy, expand the economy through new job opportunities for the foreseeable future, in addition to other economic activities. On top of that locally produced energy will go long way in the goal of making the USA less dependent on imported oil with these cheap energy sources.

Congress should look into whether such measures which have such extensive adverse effects on the people's cost of living are worth continuing or giving preferential support. For instance, some farmers have reduced the production of such crops like soya beans in favor of planting corn because the corn price is high after being subsidized by Congress.

(H) Overview Chapter

We have so far mentioned problems and issues the USA has left hanging in these last chapters. We have shown that economic and social issues have either received little attention or have been dealt with in a piecemeal manner. The main problem why these issues remain unsolved is because of political intrigue. Political considerations appear to have overridden other solutions in the best interests of the USA. The main strategies for the political parties are to win the next elections and be in power. Compromise is considered a weakness and the party in power discourages any ideas or participation by the opposition party

It is therefore important for the parties to opt for positions that put America first. They should stop bickering over good ideas just because they have been introduced by another party. A lot of time is unnecessarily wasted debating unimportant issues. By the end of the four-year tenure, they find that no significant legislation has been achieved. This is a big waste of public resources and chances for economic and social development

The sad reality is that America is busy bickering, while the rest of the world is quickly narrowing the economic and political gap between them and the USA. These fast-growing countries include Russia, China, India, Korea, Japan, Brazil, and so many others. They have made a lot of progress and they are now in a position to answer back America because the USA is no longer the economic and political giant. Even international terrorism also has taken advantage of these lapses and is now an important negative issue in world affairs. America is increasingly no longer in a position to bully the rest of the world and dictate to them what they should do. One of the Turkish political leaders recently remarked that being an ally of the USA does not mean taking orders from Washington.

Washington must therefore change its foreign policy from being the bullying master to being the senior partner in this new world order. The USA must listen to the other points of view from other countries and be willing to compromise. It appears that the arrogance of the political parties in USA which does not encourage talking and making compromises with each one another , has spilt over into foreign relationships with the rest of the world. USA thinks it can dictate policies and demond the rest of the to doing things whole sale. If all countries of the world treated each other in a mature polite but firm way, then the world would be a much better and peaceful place to live in.

The USA alone, therefore, is no longer in a position to control what is happening in the rest of the world. In the next chapter, we shall examine in depth the current foreign policy and how it can be improved upon. Good foreign policy is vital for world peace and prosperity. This was demonstrated by the Reagan strategies which produced positive results for world democracy, peace, and economic development, during and well beyond this Presidency.

106) Foreign Affairs

(i) General Remarks

There have been moments when the USA, the positive foreign policy paid off in its favor and they were able to influence world affairs. For instance during the tenure of J.F Kennedy, and LBJ the world seemed to be heading towards world peace and economic development. During this time, there was a world cultural revolution and most people wanted to see what they could do for their country and the world community at large, other than what the USA or the world could do for them. The same spirit continued through the reign of LBJ and many people wanted to participate not for money alone but to be among those who made the world a better place. The peace corps of that time was a symbol of this policy.

Another time when the US policy proved to be successful was during the presidency of Ronald Reagan. His policy of being able to negotiate with others but at the same time try to keep the US strong succeeded and culminated in the meltdown of the cold war, and the collapse of the USSR and its communist allied states. These developments succeeded in assuring world peace, economic and social development during the Reign of Ronald R., G. W. Bush, and Bill Clinton. The former USSR and China all seemed to embrace the free market concept and they also experienced tremendous economic growth, especially in China. The world came to respect the USA as the leader of the new world order. The Middle East also seemed to embrace peace, and most of them made tremendous economic and social development. The USA rating in the Middle East showed a positive trend during this period and everything seemed to be moving forward.

The USA however, after some time started making mistakes. Instead of taking advantage of these developments to make many friends and develop allies, they gradually became intolerant, uncompromising and they lacked long-term strategies, beyond Ronald Reagan. This arrogance provided fertile ground for opposing forces and terrorists. Indeed this ended in the rebirth and acceptance of communism, on the left, and the emergence of defiant autocratic regimes such as Venezuela, N. Korea, and Iran, etc. In addition, came the growing influence and acceptance of international terrorism. All these forces have now taken root and have become the center stage of the anti-USA platform. The world is once again at crossroads between war and peace, between free-market forces concepts and government-controlled economies.

The USA and free-market world have been weakened further by the recent 2007 economic meltdown. What is also disturbing is that the USA in fact compromised the free market concepts by nationalizing private enterprises and thereafter adopting other socialist-like policies such as instituting many controlling agencies and regulations. No wonder leaders like Hugo Chavez and Fidel Castro are celebrating because what they have been advocating for and practicing all along has now come to pass in the USA. The other problem the US is facing is that it is now fighting two wars since the terror attack on the US on September 11th, 2001. This means that there are fewer resources, manpower, and time to devote to other world issues.

As a result, the US appears to no longer have a long-term strategic foreign policy and they have shifted to a policy of reacting to world events as they unfold. The biggest losers seem to be the emerging Democracies because they do not have much to offer of strategic interest and importance to the USA and yet they need a lot of assistance for them to keep developing economically and also maintain the democratic political gains. For instance, the situation of Darfur in Sudan has been sidelined despite the fact that there is a lot of suffering and many people have lost their lives. It appears this is because Darfur has nothing much to offer strategically. It seems countries with resources are not willing to help. The people of Darfur and other African communities were expecting that the first black USA president would mount his horse and shining armor and come to rescue his brethren. However, they soon came to realize that he could not help because USA hands were tied mainly because of fighting two wars concurrently. Secondly, there is no mood in the USA to start another engagement. On top of that Darfur does not have any strategic importance to USA interests.

Unfortunately, even the UN has been unable to act because the US and the rest of European countries who normally can endorse, influence, and contribute logistics were unable to come forward and assist in full force or even commit to providing the necessary logistics including financial assistance. Despite so many UN resolutions on Darfur, the Sudanese leaders were able to ignore the world community and the whole world is just looking. Even the African Union is unable to act because it has no resources of its own to implement the UN resolutions. The African Unions' hands are also tied with the fact that they agreed to no interference in each other's internal affairs. This is a big weakness within the African Union. They need to revisit this policy. The people of Darfur continue to suffer but in the case of Libya instant action was taken.

(II) Use Of Resources

(a). The anti-free market forces are able to use little resources but can influence events on the world stage. These terrorist and communist leaning groups have a way of aligning themselves with the ordinary people and they provide them with everyday solutions by giving assistance to these individuals and communities. These organizations provide the people with education, medical, food, and other ordinary needs. In this way, the population comes to identify themselves with these groups and they look at the USA and other western countries as the aggressors. This is what the USA and its allies have failed to do. The USA spends a lot of the aid money on military aid and amorphous projects. They have friends only at government levels but not with the people in these emerging countries.

While it is true that the US is currently militarily over-committed and as a result has fewer resources to commit to the rest of its foreign obligations, there is a need for them to use what they have in a more efficient and effective manner. The current US government foreign policy is governed mainly by military-economic and strategic interests. In pursuance of these interests, the USA seems to put more emphasis on political, military, and intelligence assistance over civilian aid. Even the bulk of the civilian aid is channeled through government to government bilateral understanding. There is hardly any direct aid to the local communities through the private sector using organizations such as international and local NGOs, churches other local community organizations, etc. In so doing the US finds itself more identified with those the governments and their military since there is little emphasis on getting themselves as nearer to the people as much as possible. That is why the USA has low ratings among most local communities whenever a survey is conducted.

The dangers with this kind of policy are that the recipient government could and usually changes by becoming corrupt, autocratic, undemocratic, etc and as a result, the government loses the support of the population. As far as the USA is concerned their hands are tied since they are now committed to supporting these now unpopular regimes. These regimes are now allies of the USA and they do what the USA wants them to do. They are in good hands on their part because of the USA's interest in wanting them to stay in power because they are their buddies. The USA is now seen to be in favor of these unpopular regimes and against the people. This can be exemplified today with examples such countries as Egypt, Zaire, Lebanon, and so many others. In all these cases the US supports the governments and their leaders unreservedly but does not help or associate themselves with the local populations.

In the case of Zaire, the USA supported the late Mobutu Sese Seko because he was their man. It has been alleged that Mobutu was on the CIA payroll. In return, Mobutu robbed his country by underselling Zaire minerals to his overseas companies and was reckoned to be worth more than the US $ 5 billion by the time he died. He is reckoned to have amassed enough resources to pay off Zaire's external debt. Many people in Zaire were left to live in poverty because there was no way they could remove Mobutu from power in a democratic way since Mobutu would deal with any dissent in a ruthless manner and had the backing of the USA as their man.

In the case of Egypt, when the population revolted against the government, the USA was looking at the military to quell the situation because they had no contact with the local people.

In contrast, the Muslim Brotherhood in Egypt has been giving the communities medical, education, and other assistance. The ordinary people are therefore with the Muslim brotherhood rather than the USA which was giving the Egyptian leader and military life support to stay in power. This was despite the fact that the regime had lost credibility. The Muslim Brotherhood is therefore poised to win elections in Egypt. It could end up being a ruthless extremist Muslim regime. Had the USA also invested in the people, the picture today in Egypt would be a different story? The USA could easily have reduced the massive military and bilateral aid to Egypt and increased the direct economic assistance to the Egyptian people.

In the case of Lebanon, Hezbollah gives the local population medical, educational, and other local aid. The local population has come to identify themselves with them because a friend in need is a friend indeed. Local people in any country usually identify themselves with whoever helps them in their simple daily needs. Hezbollah now has a political grip over Lebanon.

Let me also mention Uganda because I have the local knowledge of how the USA foreign aid works there. In Uganda, the USA is the biggest donor mainly through budget support programs through bilateral agreements between the USA and Uganda government. However, there is almost nothing on the ground that the local people can directly identify with the USA. The US Ambassador's fund in Uganda is about US$100,000 a year and this cannot go very far as donor support. When the ambassador donated iron sheets worth US$14,000 for a school in my local area, there was so much jubilation among the local people because the aid helped to put a roof over the students' heads as many of them were studying under mango trees and most of the time could hardly hear what the teachers were telling them. This also helped them to study without interruption during the rainy season. Because of this little aid ,the local people started recognizing the USA as a partner and friend. There was participation between the USA and the people. The USA can therefore spend little money to make friends and get support from local communities and the results are enormous.

(b). Ronald Reagan was effective in assisting emerging African countries. He declared that emergency aid for Africa should be procured in Africa. This helped the local business people and the farmers to thrive. Local industries making blankets, cooking oil, etc started making good business. On top of that, countries producing maize, beans, and other products also started doing good business as this helped the farmers to sell their crops. As a result, auxiliary businesses and all sorts of jobs were created around these activities. Unfortunately, this policy was reversed after the presidency of Ronald Reagan. USA started supplying emergency aid directly from USA stocks in a bid to sell America abroad. These are small examples of what good policies can do for the local populations and in the end, produce amazing results in these emerging economies.

(c). Another example of imbalanced aid was this 10 million dollars aid program in Uganda towards the AIDS initiatives in the early 1990s. This was at the time when there was little knowledge about the disease and many people were dying day and night. Local people could not afford the then-existing expensive drugs. This program was channeled through the Ugandan government. 50% of the money was spent on administrative expenses; US$4.7 million was spent on AIDS awareness and sensitization through the media, music, dance, and drama, etc. Only US$300,000 dollars was allocated to help people with HIV. Such a program could not be seen as helpful to the main target group who were at the time dying daily in big numbers. A little more money could have been allocated to supplement the treatment of the people themselves and also assist their orphans to attend school etc. The people would have been pleased and would be remembering the USA today as they remember President G.W. Bush. G.W Bush's aid initiatives went directly to the concerned communities although once again was channeled through the government. Although as expected, there were mishaps in the global fund to a certain extent the program has helped people get treatment and to live longer. Government to government bilateral aid is ok but can be wasteful and unrealistic to what is on the ground and solutions thereof.

(d) The USA could emulate countries such as Denmark who use their aid more effectively. For instance in Uganda, DANIDA was providing aid by digging boreholes to provide water to local communities and supplying essential drugs for the common diseases directly to the communities. In my county, for instance, they dug 100 boreholes and supplied essential drugs to local dispensaries and clinics down to village levels. In turn, the local people contributed by digging latrines for their households, and this contributed to better clean water. As a result dispensaries and clinics which were always full of patients with waterborne diseases all of a sudden became deserted because the waterborne causes had been eradicated with the help of the Danish program. Such programs can be effective and popular among the population whether or not the regimes are corrupt, undemocratic, and ruthless. When the time comes to remove these bad regimes, the US can rest be assured that they have supporters and friends right from the grass-roots level. Had such a policy been applied in Egypt, the USA would not be looking to the Egyptian army as the only option to stop the Muslim brotherhood from a possible takeover of the country if free and fair elections were held today. These radical groups such as the Muslim Brotherhood and Hezbollah, etc use very little resources but have been able to influence local communities compared to what the USA spends as bilateral civil and military aid. As a future strategic measure, the USA should look at this strategy as a measure that will produce excellent results.

(e). It is advisable for the USA to use a double-barrel approach in its foreign policy by giving aid through military and bilateral government arrangement, but more importantly by also giving direct grants to the local communities. This would be an effective, efficiently and profitable utilization of USA foreign aid. The USA has been tempted to ignore democratic standards in giving aid to such corrupt aid receiving countries. These leaders are encouraged to ignore their people because they know that the USA will keep them in power no matter what. These leaders' allegiance is more towards the USA rather than to their people. It is alleged that on many occasions the USA has gone to the extent of picking future political leaders for these aid receiving countries. It is also said that the USA controls these leaders so much that they even write questions and provide answers to these leaders for issues that are important to the USA. It is common knowledge that the USA publically talks about regime change whenever they are unhappy with certain leaders. If some other leaders talked about regime change in the USA, I am sure that there will be an uproar in Washington.

106

(II) INTERNATIONAL TERRORISM

The other issue that is threatening US foreign policy is the emergence and prominence of international terrorism. This menace of terrorism has unfortunately also taken root in our homeland. In addition to terrorism, there is also the emergence of other terror groups such as drug dealers and Somali-type pirates. All these features are threatening democracy and world peace both in the USA and the world at large. These kinds of unruly groups are not new. In the past, we had such groups as the Red Brigades who were causing havoc to general peace but were defeated by the determination of the population and the concerned governments of that time. The difference today, however, is that some of the terror organizations such as Al Qaeda are openly supported and encouraged by some countries.

What also is important to note is that these groups are willing to put up long drawn fights. Al Qaeda for instance has now linked up with the Taliban in Afghanistan waiting for the promised withdrawal of US forces beginning July 2011 and then strike hard. They know that usually US cuts and runs as they did after the Gulf war. This is when the Kurdish people of northern Iraq were abandoned overnight. It is therefore important for the US and the world community to be prepared to confront these groups by hanging in there.

There are several things which the USA can do in order to get rid of the terror menace.

1. HUMAN INTELLIGENCE

One way to defeat these terror groups is the greater use of human intelligence instead of relying almost entirely on wiretapping, other electronic means, and military options. Saddam Hussein was captured as a result of human intelligence. Gen. Petraeus won the Iraq war partly because he dealt with the general public which helped him defeat the enemy. If the population is with you it is easy to uproot the enemy.

2. GLOBAL ACTIONS ON TERRORISM;

It is important for the US to get the general support of all countries through the United Nations so that a general effort is made to eradicate these terror groups and deny them sanctuary. The United States should take punitive measures against countries that give sanctuary and support terrorism. The USA should generally not be too friendly to countries that encourage and condone the actions of terrorists.

3. USA HOME LAND ACTION ON TERRORISM ;

Here in the US ordinary people sometimes want to give information on what they think is a threat, likely threat, or circumstances that might lead to US insecurity. The intelligence organs however show no interest in what these people have to say. They dismiss them on grounds that the information given does not tell them the exact location of where they can instantly find and arrest the terrorists. They are not interested in the information that can be investigated and could in the future avert terror actions against the USA. It may be prudent to have a desk dealing with ordinary people, assess such information, and take appropriate action. This can help the USA in dealing with potential insecurity cases before they hatch.

106 (III) Treatment Of Undemocratic Regimes

The strange thing is that currently, the USA seems to be more willing to accommodate, give prominence, and audience to such undemocratic countries such as Iran, N. Korea, and Venezuela, Cuba, etc some of which President Bush referred to as "The axis of evil". The shift of US policy to appease these countries on the pretext that they are talking to the enemy seems to have sidelined US allies and friends of the free world. It appears that it is easier for Chavez, Mahmoud Ahmadinejad, and Kim Jong IL to have the ears of the White House rather than the USA allies and other neutral but pro-free market countries of the free world. It seems that their loyalty to the ideals of the free world is taken for granted and therefore there is no need to give prominence to such important relationships.

When we have the UN meetings, all the news media is concentrated on what Chavez, Mahmoud Ahmadinejad, and other notorious leaders including Gaddafi have said or about to say. They hardly talk about what the good leaders have contributed to so many good deeds leading to world peace, human development, etc.

While it is generally acknowledged that bad news is good news for the media, it is the duty of the US foreign policy desk to give prominence and mention the good things being done by the not so notorious Leaders of countries of the free world. This is important because the rest of the world is anxious to know what can be done and what is being done to make the world a more peaceful and prosperous place to live in.

Other than the western world, many of the new democracies have contributed to world peace and democracy. They have produced strong good leaders such as Gandhi, Nelson Mandela, and Jomo Kenyatta who led their countries to true Democracy without seeking despite having been tortured, imprisoned, mistreated, etc by their Colonial masters. These leaders have helped the emerging democracies stand against these anti-democratic forces and have helped to show that we can have a world of no revenge

106 (V) Re-Adjustment Of Usa Foreign Policy

It is important for the USA to re-establish long-term goals such as those developed by Ronald Reagan if the USA has any chance of keeping its leadership role in the world. The US policy should be easily identified and should not keep shifting from situation to situation. The US for instance went in full support of the rebels in Libya and joined the rest of the world in stopping Gadaffi from massacring the people in the Benghazi area of Libya. This is in spite of unconfirmed reports that some of the anti-Gaddafi forces were Al Qaeda supporters whom the USA is fighting worldwide. The whole situation is delicate and complicated. One only hopes that you do not remove one devil and then encourage another to take advantage.

When it came to Syria the US did not come out in full support of the demonstrators who are fighting against the Syrian brutal régime. The USA instead gave the excuse that this was because Syria was helping the USA to fight against Al Qaeda. Syria up to now continues to imprison and mercilessly kill hundreds of people who oppose the dictatorial Syrian regime. All this makes it difficult to know what the USA foreign policy is all about. The whole policy is full of total confusion. The USA should evolve long-term foreign policies based more on principles other than purely on economic and security interests. It should be a policy the rest of the world can read. This in the long run will generate more world peace and prosperity. The USA should also consider its allies as partners and not its satellite states, who are there to sing their masters' voice.

CHAPTER 10

107. THE WAY FORWARD

We now start looking at what future direction the USA should be shaping. We shall begin by dealing with the current situation before engaging in future directions, policies, and options.

(1) CURRENT STATUS QUO;

First of all, it is important to look at the current political setup in the country. After the 2008 elections, a new phenomenon has emerged on the political scene.

(i). On the extreme right-wing of the Republican Party, the Tea Party has evolved into a strong extreme right political group. The group argues that the Republican Party had lost the conservative values and basic principles of the party. They advocate that the principle of small government, less expenditure, and other conservative principles should be revamped and adhered to. During the health care debate most of the tea baggers, as they were often referred to by the Democrats, went to town hall meetings and advocated for the overhaul of the health care bill as had been presented to Congress at that time. By the mid-term 2010 elections, the Tea Party had gained prominence and become so strong that they were able to field their own candidates. Indeed some of the Tea party supported candidates made it to congress. They have now a strong lobby within the Republican Party. They are now pushing for right-wing ideas and they are expecting the country to follow. There is however a possibility that they could be going too far by trying to push the country too far to the right. There is a fear that this could hurt the Republican Party in the 2012 elections especially among the independent voters who are normally the swing voters of elections these days. In fact, some of the Republican Legislatures in Washington are now afraid to take positions that may not be in line with those of the right-wing of the Party.

The tea party members of congress have even started a caucus of their own to advocate for the main tea party ideas of small government, less spending, and reduction of the national debt. Their ideas on other issues such as immigration, health care however seem to be too far to the right and the unfortunate thing is that they do not seem to be willing to listen or compromise with other positions. Recently when former President GW Bush was asked to comment on immigration, he warned that the US might drift into isolationism if they are not willing to listen to other ideas about the issue. He was immediately attacked by the Tea party advocates and the conservative media for holding and giving an opinion that was contrary to the tea party's position. It was as if he had committed a crime for giving his own honest views. It is important that for the good of democracy and finding solutions to America's problems that the Tea Party advocates must try and listen to other people with differing views. They should be prepared to compromise and assist in finding common ground and solutions to these issues. If they are not willing to listen to other views and compromise on issues, the politics might drift further into more into a more serious political grid spearheaded by the extreme wings of both parties.

(ii). On the other side of the political spectrum, we have the Democratic Party also has its own setup. Recently the extreme left wing of the Democratic Party organized themselves into a block of their own to counter the growing influence of the tea party. They were led by people like Ben Jones and they organized a big concert in Washington to express their cause. The trade unions who contributed over 500 million dollars to the 2008 Democratic Party presidential elections have also taken center stage in the activities of the party. The president of the SEIU is said to have visited the white house not less than 23 times since the democrats came to power in 2008. The Trade Unions are said to have a great influence on the Democrat Party policies and they influence legislation issues in Congress. They have been allegations that the health care act and the stimulus act were products of the trade union's influence in conjunction with the far-left wing of the Democratic Party. There is a rift that has developed between the far-left group and right-leaning legislators of the Democratic Party commonly known as the "blue dogs." The far left does not seem to be consulting with the blue dogs over legislative and policy issues.

The political situation, therefore, appears to be that the extreme left led by the Trade Unions and extreme left-wing advocates have a big influence on the Democratic Party while the Tea Party has taken center stage in the Republican Party. The two parties have a big task to re-establish control of their parties because the solutions to the American problems might be in jeopardy unless both parties try to move to the center, in order to find common ground on important legislative issues.

108. THE FUTURE

In the previous chapters of this book, we tried to highlight issues that were long outstanding but needed urgent attention, especially by Congress. If these recommendations which we have made are adopted and implemented, then many of economic, political and social problems would have, as a consequence, been addressed to a great extent. The following are some of the possible positive results as which can arise if the recommendations are implemented

(a) Jobs;

Since many of the outstanding issues would have been addressed, the most burning issues as of today such as the creation of a conducive atmosphere for job creation opportunities would have been given a good jump start. This is mainly because the private sector and the business community would now be able to plan for future business opportunities and therefore be able to make sustainable and predictable long-term strategic business plans. All this would mean the creation of long-term jobs and expansion of the economy.

(b) The National Debt;

The other important issue which would have been largely addressed is the nation's debt. The various cost-saving measures would have reduced the current deficit levels and therefore had an impact on the extent of the national debt.

(c) Budget control ;

The savings made by implementing the programs would automatically reduce the deficit and budget size. After this meaningful future adjustments can be made based on known data.

These measures would at least have started turning the economy in the right direction thus making the USA's economic future look be very bright.

There are many suggestions on how to propel the economy further in the right direction including tackling the issue of the size of the national debt. Some of the suggestions which appear to have popular sentiments with the population may not necessarily be the best options in solving the economic problems.

For instance, there is a republican economic recovery idea that calls for budget spending levels to be scaled back to the same size that of the Ronald Reagan administration. This may not be the best solution because the situation and budgetary demands of today have changed since the era of the Ronald Regan administration. For instance, the USA is currently fighting two wars and has to find money to spend on them. There is also the 2010 Health Care Act which has just started being implemented. Nobody knows the full financial impact of the Act until it is wholly implemented. The economy is just beginning to recover from the 2007 recession and different solutions might be needed to recover the economy back to the levels before the recession started and beyond.

I agree that Congress and the Executive must try and reduce the current budget spending levels because the country cannot keep on borrowing indefinitely to cover these budget shortfalls. However, this must be done in a planned and thoughtful manner.

There is a tendency and general belief that just advocating for the opposite view or going in the opposite direction of what is on the ground provides the right answer to the problem. That line of argument is always popular because what is on the ground appears to be failing and therefore unpopular with the population. In reality, this is like engaging a reverse gear while the vehicle is still running fast as such, a sudden move might instead damage the vehicle. The best way is to either stop the vehicle and then engage in the reverse gear or slow down and then turn the vehicle in the direction you want it to face.

The same goes for the economy and budgeting. Even if you feel the economy is moving in the wrong direction, itis better to slow down, plan and then move in that direction by implementing the right corrective measures.

We now move onto some of the corrective measures which can lead the USA to a bright future.

109 BUDGETING AND RESTRUCTURING

This would involve looking at the current budget spending levels of all the departments and comparing them to the spending levels during the time when the USA last produced a budget surplus. Then continue to examine the spending percentage increases/reductions in spending for each department between the two periods. The next thing needed is to evaluate what caused these particular percentage increases/reductions in comparison to the previous levels. If such increases in spending are not justifiable then immediate corrective action must be taken. This is the best way of evaluating and getting the problem right without hurting the economy. Any unjustified increase must be immediately dropped save for the inflation factor.

HEALTHCARE;

(A) As for healthcare we have dealt with these Social programs and made a wide range of recommendations. The major effects of these changes would include.

> i. Adoption of the grants system for Medicaid
>
> ii. Savings through a reduction in waste and frauds
>
> iii. Solve social security problems
>
> iv. Amalgamate healthcare activities in a one-stop-shop center.
>
> v. Introduction of a national sales tax for medical or healthcare activities. This ensures that Healthcare is universal since everyone contributes to the system. The system can co-exist with others, but this ensures that nobody is deprived of medical treatment. Universal Healthcare can have advantages ;

a . Healthy people lose less working man-hours

b. Healthy people have a higher production capacity and they tend to live longer, providing the country many more years of trained labor. Spending money on keeping people healthy is worth every penny spent. There is a saying that prevention is better than cure. The suggested consumer tax is paid for by everybody including non-US nationals, visitors, etc, all contribute to their well-being while in the USA. It has been suggested that the overwhelming majority of the people would prefer such a tax to be put in place so that basic and specialized health services are put in place especially for those who cannot afford some of the expensive health care insurance. There is a misconception that without insurance cover there can be no healthcare treatment. The current healthcare act is bad because it forces everybody to purchase insurance or no treatment. Even with cars, not every piece of insurance covers accidents and car repairs. It is therefore high time to release the people from the healthcare insurance syndrome. People can pay taxes to cover their body repairs without going through insurance, especially those who cannot afford to purchase insurance including visitors illegal's, etc. Those will be covered by the proposed health consumer healthcare national sales tax. A surveyor better still a referendum can be made to prove whether this point is what most people would like to have for their own healthcare. A sales tax would help them do this without much stress on their pockets.

DEPARTMENT OF DEFENCE

(B) As far as the Department of Defense is concerned considerations beyond security should be looked into. These would include defense arms sales receipts and how much defense research contributes to science. It is said that the USA is the largest arms dealer and therefore could be making export receipts for the country. This is provided that most of these exports are not part of the foreign military aid. If the bulk of export is military aid is then it would be necessary to make major reductions in Defense expenditure without compromising defense capabilities.

EDUCATION DEPARTMENT

(C) The Education department has been cited as having many duplicated programs all over the place which are more or less doing the same thing. It is important to rationalize all these programs so that savings can be made. For instance, this would mean a lot of savings which can be transferred to other needy areas or in the reduction of the national debt and budget deficits or improve services within the Department.

It is important to note that the Catholic Church spends approximately $6000 per child per annum on education and yet the public schools spend twice as much. Charter schools spend somewhere in between. What is even more difficult to understand is the catholic run schools and charter schools produce better grades and their students are more disciplined. In John Stossel's program 'stupid in America' Charter schools are not only cheaper than public schools but they also have control over the hiring of and firing of teachers, and other personnel in their schools. According to the same program it can also cost up to US $ 250,000 to just attempt to fire a bad teacher who is not doing a reasonable job of teaching in the public schools. This is because the trade unions have made it almost impossible to discipline any teacher. According to one union boss in Washington DC he said that teachers should not be fired but corrected and trained.

John Stossel also interviewed a former school chancellor in Washington DC Micheal Lee and she is said to have said that she had to find a way to fire hundreds of teachers because in her opinion they were not doing their work. She is also said to have remarked that many students were skipping some classes because they did not like certain bad teachers. Unfortunately, she had to leave her assignment before she could assess the results because her appointing authority lost the political office as he was not re-elected. All this goes on to show that getting good grades and discipline in public schools needs a lot of attention and restructuring and all this can be done with reduced spending.

What is strange is that the Department of Education has refused to cooperate with the Catholic Church and Charter School Administrations to see where improvements and savings can be made without compromising standards. Such savings would go a long way to reduce the budget deficit and national debt or if needed provide better facilities for schools and teachers

CLEAN ENERGY VENTURE INVESTMENT PROGRAMS

(D) Although the recovery act allocated $60billion for the going green initiatives, the expenditure has not proved to be so successful because few jobs have been created. The main aim of the recovery act was job creation. The cost per job created under the green energy program runs in thousands and thousands of dollars making this sector a poor return and utilization of tax payer's money, especially at the time of recession when the public cannot afford this type of experimentation. Maybe Congress should have been more serious when dealing with the components of the recovery act since unemployment is still above 9%. This program, in the opinion of many people, should have been dealt with as a research grants issue other than a venture capital item. The program was supposed to generate millions of high-tech jobs, but some studies say that this is not the case while others claim that over a million jobs have been created.

There are claims that there is another US $500 million allocated for research and development of green jobs and this also had anticipated creating 80,000 stimulus green jobs but up to now, only 8000 have been created. The study further estimates that it costs approximately US $ 374,000 to create one green job. It also claimed that Green jobs energy costs around US $ 210 per mega unit compared with the US $ 60 per mega unit for gas.

Another study has revealed that to police all these green regulations as required by EPA rules would cost about US $ 21 billion and would require in the region of 250,000 people to be employed for this exercise. The country cannot afford such expenditure at this time. Too many regulations might even kill jobs such as those of small business owners who can hardly afford to comply with all these complicated numerous regulations.

At this critical time of economic recovery, it is better as a policy to implement programs based on reality and economic advantage other than those based on hope and fantasy. This is especially so if one is to replace the other. It is only logical to plan the economy using the best cheapest resources and spend money on research for the best cheapest energy sources of the future

(110) Tax Reform

This would involve the following major areas

a. Reversal of corporation tax loopholes.

It is important to eliminate all the selective tax loopholes that are embedded in the current tax code because they cause a lot of imbalance in the economy especially since corporate tax rates are some of the highest in the world. Tax credits that are not universal for all corporations in the same category give an unfair advantage to those corporations which manage to get them granted.

It is not surprising that some lawmakers, media commentators, etc keep complaining that corporations such as oil companies eg Exxon, and other corporations such as General Electric hardly pay any corporation tax. This is because they have managed to use their influence through special interests and lobbyists to get congress to pass these unfair special favors for them. If this is true it is not fair to the general public and to the corporations who pay the full tax. Congress should avoid this animal farm kind of concessions and unfair treatment since it is vital to level the ground. Everybody must be treated in a fair way if the spirit of fair competition is to be observed. Capitalism cannot work well without open fair competition.

It is true that these executives are concerned with improving the bottom line of their corporations so that they can pay higher dividends to the shareholders and claim bonuses for themselves but they must not do so at the expense of the ordinary person, and other players in the business industry. Some of these companies are sitting on billions of dollars both here and abroad and it is therefore not logical to give them these concessions. In any case, many of these corporations are not going to spend the money. They just want to build their bank balances and reserves. This is the opposite when you give tax credits to an ordinary person who lives paycheck to paycheck because the money that person saves or receives will be spent immediately thus increasing demand for goods and services. This will in the end stimulate and further expand the economy.

The problem with these greedy corporations is that they want to make more money every year even when their activities are not expanding. They must therefore be extracting this extra profit from the taxpayer by charging higher prices to the consumer and or through squeezing employees by extracting more work from them without extra remuneration or with a reduced workforce and no overtime They forget that this cannot go on forever because eventually the consumers will either give up buying the products, make noise or react in so many different ways. This is not good for the capitalist economy in the long run. Equal treatment in the tax code is therefore a vital component to the success of the free market economy system. Congress must therefore regularize this issue as a matter of urgency. If this was done the economy would immediately react favorably.

b. Review and streamline subsidies ;

Subsidies can be good and or bad depending on what they are supposed to achieve. The most glaring subsidy which we mentioned earlier was ethanol. The subsidy is said to be partly responsible not only for higher consumer prices of dairy products such as meat and milk but also transport costs and higher prices across the board.

It is reasoned that the subsidy gives incentives to farmers to plant corn because they are guaranteed high prices. This is to guarantee enough production of corn for ethanol production in order to comply with current regulations which require a certain percentage of ethanol to be blended in the pump gas. Businesses that need and use corn in various other cases such as the feeding of animals are forced to pay these high corn prices and in the end, they have no alternative but to increase the prices of their end products to the consumer.

Research has found that the cost of production for ethanol is 50 cents higher, per gallon than gas. The price of gas, therefore, has to be hiked by the factor of 20-30 cents per gallon of gas thus making transport costs unnecessary higher. Subsidizing uneconomic businesses, therefore, does not make economic sense and adversely affects the economy. This matter should be immediately investigated and rectified without delay. It is not good for the economy to support such adverse economic activities which have a negative impact on the budget and the economy because it is the ordinary taxpayers to pay the price for any adverse economic consequences.

The country should not circumvallate the present cheaper energy sources in favor of other currently expensive alternatives which still need further research. One has to look at South Dakota today and see the reality. Their unemployment rate is between 3-4% much lower than the national average rate of 9%. One does not need a rocket scientist to know where to invest their resources at this moment.

Recently I heard an advert on the radio which claimed that solar power was cheaper than the current power rates. They claimed that installation of the equipment was free and there is also a US $ 700 rebate. If this is true bravo and we should all rush to install solar energy since this would be good for the people and the economy. I just hope that the taxpayer is not footing the bill for all these solar incentives. I do not have enough information to verify this good news from solar.

c. Review of current tax rate   We shall start by discussing recent tax rate changes in the USA. We shall take a direct quote from the Article " Guess who really pays the Taxes" item 5 and 6 by Stephen Moore.

This can be found at www.american.com/archive/2007/ november-decembermagazine-contents. and it reads as it follows:
5). What has happened to tax rates in America over the last several decades?

They've fallen. In the early 1960s, the highest marginal income tax rate was a stunning 91 percent. That top rate fell to 70 percent after the Kennedy-Johnson tax cuts and remained there until 1981.

Then Ronald Reagan slashed it to 50 percent and ultimately to 28 percent after the 1986 Tax Reform Act. Although the federal tax rate fell by more than half, total tax receipts in the 1980s doubled from $517 billion in 1981 to $1,030 billion in 1990. The top tax rate rose slightly under George H. W. Bush and then moved to 39.6 percent under Bill Clinton. But under George W. Bush it fell again to 35 percent. So what's striking is that, even as tax rates have fallen by half over the past quarter-century, taxes paid by the wealthy have increased. Lower tax rates have made the tax system more progressive, not less so. In 1980, for example, the top 5 percent of income earners paid only 37 percent of all income taxes. Today, the top 1 percent pay that proportion, and the top 5 percent pay a whopping 57 percent.

6). What is the economic logic behind these lower tax rates? ;

As legend has it, the famous "Laffer Curve" was first drawn by economist Arthur Laffer in 1974 on a cocktail napkin at a small dinner meeting attended by the late Wall Street Journal editor Robert Bartley and such high-powered policymakers as Richard Cheney and Donald Rumsfeld. Laffer showed how two different rates—one high and one low—could produce the same revenues since the higher rate would discourage work and investment. The Laffer Curve helped launch Reaganomics here at home and ignited a frenzy of tax-cutting around the globe that continues to this day. It's also one of the simplest concepts in economics: lowering the tax rate on production, work, investment, and risk-taking will spur more of these activities and will often produce more tax revenue rather than less.

Since the Reagan tax cuts, the United States has created some 40 million new jobs—more than all of Europe and Japan combined. It is said that US corporation tax rates are some of the highest in the world. It is also strongly suggested that the corporation tax rate should be reduced to about 25% and that all corporations should pay the revised rate which will level the ground for all corporations. The measure will also as a result encourage corporations to be less tempted to evade paying taxes. The reduction will also encourage capital inflows as corporations will find it more attractive to invest in the United States.

As for federal income for individuals, there are suggestions that the threshold for starting to pay as you earn taxes should be raised to at least to US $50,000 per person. This is because the cost of living has been raising and therefore the above changes are necessary.

The tax refund system could stay as it helps ordinary people to make compulsory savings which they get refunded at the beginning of the following year. This enables the taxpayers to buy items that they would have never had normally saved for. Tax rates for individuals after the US$ 50,000 threshold should also remain gradual so that people who earn just above the threshold should not be punished. The maximum for those earning high incomes should also not exceed 30% in any case.

I do not believe that ordinary people who do not pay federal income tax do not contribute to the economy. This is because whatever they earn is spent on goods and services on which they are taxed at both Federal and State levels. Since they spend almost all they earn, there is nothing they have evaded because they do not have much remaining taxable income. Whatever they have spent has been taxed in one way or another. The tax policy should reflect this reality. There is a big disparity between low-income earners and high-income earners. At least the high-income earners have a way of avoiding paying some of the taxes using loopholes in the tax codes.

(III) REVIEW OF ECONOMIC POLICIES

It is important and necessary for Congress and the Executive to institute policies that are in line with the economic principles of the free market economy. Measures that are not in line with these principles will gradually and eventually negatively affect the performance of the economy. The economy will not perform as anticipated by the free market economic market principles and then the people will start blaming and doubting the system. The people might not realize that foreign bodies have been introduced into the system and that is why the economy has started stalling. The free market policy should not be confused with the obligation of the state to provide services to the people. Some of the services are better provided at the State or Federal level as in the case of the U.S because it is more difficult to handle such issues as individuals.

That is why people elect a government to take care of such issues which are better dealt with as a community. Some of these major items include Defense, Education, Energy, Healthcare, Transport, and of late Research. All these plus others can only be done on a collective basis. It does not mean that the Federal or State governments have to run all these services as public entities. Many of these services can better be contracted to the private sector which can run them more efficiently and at a cheaper price. For instance, Lockheed Martin, Boeing, etc provide armaments, etc to the Department of Defense because they can do it more efficiently than the department itself. However, it is not prudent or advisable for the fighting men and women to emanate from the private sector because it is vital that these men and women give allegiance to the country they are fighting for, other than the private sector.

There was a time when there were professional private armies but they did not prove to conform to the political ethics that is normally required.

Therefore the Federal Government and States can use local private partnerships to execute these programs on behalf of the people. This is because, as already mentioned, bureaucracy tends to be slow and less efficient.

What services should be run by the Federal Government or States using the private sector is the main issue. For instance, in the case of Healthcare, the Republican and Democratic Legislators can not agree what is the best way to serve the people. The Republicans prefer an individual approach through insurance companies. The Democrats prefer government public-run healthcare services. The best way is to allow all the different systems to co-exist just like the school system where you have public, private, charter, religious, etc educational institutions functioning alongside one another. I would prefer public healthcare services to be contracted and run by the private sector. Details of how this can work are dealt with separately

Capitalism does not mean that country abandons its social and important concerns and responsibilities to the general public. They collect money from the people mainly to provide basic services that can best be done collectively by society other than individually. These services as already mentioned include Security, Education, and Health. These services do not necessarily have to be performed by public servants as they can be hired out to the private sector if that can be done more cheaper and more efficiently. The Departments of Defense hire out many of its needs to the private sector.

We should now look at other issues which need review ;

I. PLANNING;

At the moment Congress and Executive do not appear to have a strategic short or long-term economic plan for the country. There is no predictable long or short-term economic plan on which the business community and public can depend as they plan their future activities. Congress and the Executive seem to be just responding to economic problems and challenges as they develop. The policies also tend to shift with whatever party is in power. The followings are examples to illustrate the lack of planned policies ;

(a) The 2007 economic bubble and housing problem ;

Public servants, economists, technocrats, planners, etc did not appear to have any solution to what was happening to the world economy and the US in particular in 2007. They, therefore, did not have ready answers on how the country would respond or prevent a situation such as the crash of the economy and the housing bubble. The government therefore resorted to ad hoc solutions when the problem erupted. There were thousands of guesses as to what caused the economic meltdown and housing bubble. In the first place, there were no major indicators of what and why this problem was not foreseen.

(b) The administration tried the following haphazard measures;

(i) The treasury asked for funds from Congress to deal with the problem. They instead used much of the funds for purposes other than those for which Congress had appropriated.

(ii) The administration allocated much of the money to corporations on a selective basis and with clear no guidelines. Such corporations as Leman Brothers and small to median companies were ignored and left in the cold. There was no policy or guidelines on how the small business owners would be helped out of the crisis. It was the only one responsible for the so-called "too big to fail" institutions and corporations.

(iii) The administration then went ahead and took over ownership of some of these private companies without clear plans or consultation with the shareholders. It appears they only dealt with the CEOs as if it is they who owned the Corporations. This was an unusual way of dealing with private enterprise businesses. Eventually, some of these Corporations went through new systems of bankruptcy procedures.

(iv) The administration flaunted existing bankruptcy laws, and guidelines, and procedures while dealing with these faltering companies. The Supreme Court took an unprecedented decision by siding with the Administration. to the detriment of the owners of the corporations. The trade unions were the main beneficiaries of what they did not legally own.

(2) Free Market System Support;

The above actions which Congress and the Administration took since the 2007 economic bubble and housing meltdown make it appear as if running of private business under the concept of the free market system is not the answer to solving America's economic problems.

(a) The way the government took over ownership of private companies instead of letting the free market system take its course has cast doubt into the concept of the free market system. The government is now running these failed companies and has injected a lot of the taxpayers' money. The impression one gets is as if the answer to the running of the business is best guaranteed and done through public ownership of the businesses, especially when adverse economic problems are involved.

No wonder leaders such as Castro and Chavez who nationalized private industries and businesses in their countries were happy because they say they were right after all since the USA was abandoning the free market concepts and doing what they had done. This is a clear example of how the USA is unprepared to deal with economic problems following the free market principles and solutions. They should be the leaders of being in support of private ownership of businesses under the free market system.

(b) Another example where the government is interfering with free-market principles is the health and Reconciliation Act of 2010. The act forces people to buy insurance whether they like it or not and fines them if they do not comply. Imposing a product on people is not a free market principle. The state should avoid making unilateral decisions on what the people should use.

(c) Let us take another example of the lighting bulbs.

The executive is in favor of the expensive long-lasting lighting bulbs, giving the reason that they are cheaper than the other types of bulbs in the long run. They are now in the process of phasing out the other types of bulbs. It is not the business of the government to decide what the people can buy or not. If people prefer buying one product or another, that is their choice. The executive should leave it to the public to make a choice among so many alternatives. A person may not want to put a lot of money upfront and then wait for twenty years to make a saving. Another may prefer to use his/her money now to buy a product when that person hopes savings will be made in the long run. All government is expected to do is to set minimum acceptable standards for the products in the free market for sale. The only way a product should replace another is by becoming more advantageous to produce.

When I was still young the countries of Uganda, Kenya, and Tanzania were still under the East Africa Community. Products made in any of the three countries were freely sold in the three partner states. Kenya used to produce a certain type of bread called Tip Top and this product was very popular in Uganda because of its quality and price. The population loved the bread and it was almost a household name.

When Uganda gained its independence the Uganda government tried to show economic independence by banning the importation of products such as Tip Top bread from being imported into Uganda. The people answered the ban by importing the product through whatever means including smuggling and the product continued to sell in Uganda even if it was now an illegal product. The only way the product lost the market was when the Uganda bakers started producing bread of similar quality and taste to Tip Top. The problem was solved without unnecessary fighting the people with unpopular and anti-free market decisions. These are the right solutions to solving problems using the free market process.

The best way for the government to do this is to ensure that the free market system is conducted under fair conditions. The USA has been practicing a capitalist free market system for the last two centuries and there is no indication that the system is failing. Therefore the long life expensive lighting bulb policy was wrong.

(d) The other basic thing the USA government should do is to ensure that there is peace, law, and order in the country. Peace is one of the pre-requisites for providing a conducive atmosphere for business to thrive. This does not mean that government should not show any concern or responsibility by having a Liaise fair policy. There must be basic rules which protect everybody while they are freely conducting their business.

If bad elements find loopholes and weaknesses in the government security system, they start developing into unruly gangs like what is happening in Somalia and Mexico.

We do not want such a situation where ordinary people have to buy protection such as they did during the days of the mafia in Italy.

(e) The government should avoid getting involved in too much regulation and telling people how things should be done because the competition is one of the other main factors which stimulate the economy and ensures fair prices. It is one of the concepts of the free market system. Once governments provide stability in a free market condition, there are no limits to economic development for that country.

D3) Private Industry Sector Jobs

Most jobs in the USA are provided and created by small-scale private enterprises. It's only logical that the government should find ways of supporting and funding these many small to medium enterprises.

The USA has been losing many industrial jobs to other countries mainly because the cost of production for industrial products in the USA is prohibitive. This is a very big challenge to the USA. The alternatives for solving the above problems are bitter pills to swallow because either USA imposes tariffs on imported goods or puts in place a quarter system. These two alternatives would end up hiking the prices of commodities and this could adversely affect the economy. The other alternative is to recommend USA enterprises to reduce costs and prices. This is almost an impossible task, as nobody would want their salaries trimmed.

The only free market solution for USA is to invest in new ideas so that USA can produce products where they have a comparative advantage. This is a grand idea which USA can adopt immediately. Ronald Regan in defense the free market system remarked that there is no way even the best central business planners can do a better job than millions of ordinary people with millions of ideas. It is these ideas which can put America to be above the rest.

At the moment people with new ideas can hardly find a ready capital source to help them develop and try out these new ideas. America can afford to put aside venture capital in form of grants and soft loans so that these millions of new ideas can become reality and ready for development or sale to the private sector. It does not involve much money since most of these new ideas would require less than US$50,000 dollars to make them ready for further development and investment. Presently, people with new ideas are left at the mercy of bogus promises of investment funding opportunities on the internet, newspaper, magazine advertisements, etc. The majority of the people end up losing even the little money they have invested while in search of these wild promises of initial venture capital funding.

If most of these millions of ideas are developed into projects, then the taxable income base will expand and there will be no limit to future economic development in this county. USA could have put itself further ahead of other countries in the competition for global development. This is the great thing that the free-market system can offer over the other systems.

Ideas have helped the US to supersede others in the development of many new products and services. Ideas such as the internet, MySpace, Facebook have been developed in the USA because of the advantages of the free market system. Such innovations are bound to impact the world for the foreseeable future. Inventions such as the computer etc have had an impact on society and nobody would have thought that this would be feasible 20 years ago. All these ideas have been developed in spite of the lack of strong government support in this area. The government should take this opportunity as soon as possible and put in place serious research and development systems so that the future of the USA's economic and political leadership can be consolidated. Research opportunities should be open and leveled for all of those who want to access them. At the moment the government is funding mostly the rich in so many sectors by providing research funding and sometimes they provide venture capital. It is recognized that all these big businesses, institutions, universities, and other institutions of learning are getting a lot of taxpayers' funds to fund research and other experimental projects.

It is only logical for the ordinary folk to be provided with the same opportunity. These millions of new ideas are therefore entitled to be given the same chance to succeed by providing them with research and venture capital grants to help them take off.

(112)THE FUTURE

(i) Political; While politics in the USA is important, it should not lag behind in the other areas of activity such as economic development.

The Executive and Congress should therefore try to avoid introducing divisive political issues when they have so many other important national issues to consider and solve.

For instance, recently, the Administration decided that they will no longer defend the defense of the marriage act of 1966 because, in their opinion, they think the act is unconstitutional. They argue that the act discriminates against gay and other same-sex relationships. By doing so the Executive is trying to render the existing law irrelevant without following the right procedures.

The general rule is that an act can only be repealed by Congress or on other various grounds by competent courts of law. What the Executive is trying to do is to usurp the powers of Congress and the Judiciary. It is an attempt to destabilize and confront the other two arms of government.

According to the constitution, it is only the judiciary that can declare an act of Congress as unconstitutional or unlawful, in accordance with the law. It is also only Congress that can make laws because legislative duties are the function of Congress. Nobody else can change or add provisions to the laws of the country other than Congress. The duty of the Executive is to implement and defend such existing laws.

What is interesting and disturbing is the legislators have made little noise about this important issue. It is a test of whether the separation of powers can stand the test of time. It is a challenge to Congress to defend their legislative responsibilities as laid down in the Constitution. Their inability to act could compromise the democratic pillars as set up in the Constitution. It is also the responsibility of the population to see that the Constitution and its provisions are upheld. People should start to address this issue with their legislators. Social media should also alert the population about such issues.

(ii) The other distractive social issue which also has failed the executive and the Congress is the problem of gay marriage. Although recently Congress and executive allowed gays to serve openly in the military, the question of gay marriage is yet to be resolved. More than 30 US states have held referenda and the people have said that marriage is a relationship between man and woman. According to the legal definition of the World English dictionary, Marriage is the state of a relationship of being husband and wife. It is a legal union-made by a man and woman to live as husband and wife. It is the state of being united to the person of the opposite sex as a husband and wife, in a legal conceal and contractual relationship. However, of late some people want to add other definitions of marriage to include those relationships such as partners of the same sex or gender. There are less than ten states which recognize same-sex marriages.

What is important is for the government is to recognize that such relationships exist. The government and especially Congress should come out with a definition of these relationships such as calling them civil partnerships and give them the same privileges as enjoyed by the marriage act. In this way, there is no way to question whether anybody is being discriminated against or not being recognized by society.

The affected people can go to civil courts and get recognized without having fights with institutions such as certain churches etc who do not want to perform same-sex union ceremonies. This definition should also able to cover all sorts of different relationships and partnerships no matter what they are. This is because nobody knows what other types of relationships will develop tomorrow and they will also demand the same rights as gays and lesbians. This could involve relationships with other species other than a man.

I have mentioned these issues because they are going to be a disruption during the next 2012 Presidential, Congressional, and state election campaigns. It is better to deal with them now so that the issue of the economy, jobs, and other important related issues can take center stage and be debated extensively during the 2012 election campaigns.

(iii) Lastly, it is important to mention that if the US is to maintain its leadership role in the world for some time to come it must invest now in the future generation.

(113) THE NEXT GENERATION

It is important for the USA to ensure that democracy and the free market concepts are carried onto the next generation. The current trend is that the younger generation is taking less and less interest in American values, way of life, and the free market concepts.

There are many reasons for these trends of which some are mentioned below:

(a) Unemployment.

See ref: www.bls.gov/web/laumstrc/html.

Unemployment rates states in USA Dec 2011

Unemployment Rates for States Monthly Rankings Seasonally Adjusted Dec. 2011ᴾ		
Rank	**State**	**Rate**
1	NORTH DAKOTA	3.3
2	NEBRASKA	4.1
3	SOUTH DAKOTA	4.2
4	NEW HAMPSHIRE	5.1
4	VERMONT	5.1
6	IOWA	5.6
7	MINNESOTA	5.7
8	WYOMING	5.8
9	UTAH	6.0
10	OKLAHOMA	6.1
11	VIRGINIA	6.2
12	KANSAS	6.3
13	HAWAII	6.6
13	NEW MEXICO	6.6
15	MARYLAND	6.7
16	LOUISIANA	6.8
16	MASSACHUSETTS	6.8
16	MONTANA	6.8
19	MAINE	7.0
20	WISCONSIN	7.1

21	ALASKA	7.3
22	DELAWARE	7.4
23	PENNSYLVANIA	7.6
24	ARKANSAS	7.7
25	TEXAS	7.8
26	COLORADO	7.9
26	WEST VIRGINIA	7.9
28	MISSOURI	8.0
28	NEW YORK	8.0
30	ALABAMA	8.1
30	OHIO	8.1
32	CONNECTICUT	8.2
33	IDAHO	8.4
34	WASHINGTON	8.5
35	ARIZONA	8.7
35	TENNESSEE	8.7
37	OREGON	8.9
38	INDIANA	9.0
38	NEW JERSEY	9.0
40	KENTUCKY	9.1
41	MICHIGAN	9.3
42	SOUTH CAROLINA	9.5
43	GEORGIA	9.7
44	ILLINOIS	9.8
45	FLORIDA	9.9
45	NORTH CAROLINA	9.9
47	DISTRICT OF COLUMBIA	10.4
47	MISSISSIPPI	10.4
49	RHODE ISLAND	10.8
50	CALIFORNIA	11.1
51	NEVADA	12.6

The unemployment rate among the young generation is relatively higher than the other groups. Among the reasons are that:—

(i) The older people are living longer and therefore working more years. This means that the younger people have to wait longer until the older generation can retire.

(ii) Employers are using automation in order to cut costs. Machines and robots are taking up jobs that were previously hired out to people. There may be more productivity but it does not reflect a similar increment in job opportunities. This leaves more people struggling for these fewer job opportunities.

(iii) Employers are loading more work on their employees as one of the money-saving measures and this has been especially so since the 2007 economic meltdown. This also does not make new employment opportunities any better since the younger generation looking for job opportunities as they come out of schools and colleges.

(iv) There are talks about making the retirement age higher when discussing social security solutions which would make the already bad status even worse.

B) OTHER REASONS;

The young generation therefore gradually feels less and less patriotic and further apart from the American system. Many young people are blaming the free capital market system as the main problem for the lack of job opportunities. Quite a number of them feel the system makes the rich richer and the poor poorer and they see that the gap between the two is widening indefinitely. Many younger people feel that they deserve a better share of the American pie and are therefore demanding services such as education and health care as an entitlement rather than as a privilege. This issue is still to be resolved by society. For me I would rather call such services essential and better done universally other than individually.

The young generation is therefore more and more willing to support and take sides with those who ask for equality in treatment and sharing of global resources. This was for instance clearly shown in the recent Wisconsin state political demonstrations as students and the younger generation demonstrated in support of their teachers, trade union, workers, and the Democratic Party lawmakers. Some students' concurred that the teachers etc were getting a raw deal from the state. When other students were asked why they were striking there were many answers given. Some did not even have any specific reason why they had joined the demonstrations. Others blamed capitalism and Wall Street, while others were in support of the trade union's right to bargain for anything including teachers' poor terms of service and conditions.

Many thought and argued that these groups were being oppressed by the capitalist system. One can see that quite a number of people no longer believe that the free market capitalist system is the answer for solving the future American economic challenges. This is also partly because they feel and believe that they are not benefiting from the system. Some do not understand the benefits of the free market system other than making the rich richer. There is therefore great need to help them experience the benefits of the free market system concept.

(C) ATTITUDE:

It is important to note that the young generation is also more liberal and more tolerant towards such issues as terrorism, gay marriage, etc and they, therefore, tend to associate with groups that are fighting for such issues.

The young generation is also less interested and less exposed to values and knowledge of such issues as American history, the constitution, and the political system versus another system, etc. They are therefore less inclined to be associated with such American values.

Furthermore, the teachers and the syllabuses in schools, universities, and other institutions tend to take more a liberal attitude on many issues including these basic values. It has been said that conservative educators are less popular with the young generation and they tend to be jeered at during their presentations. It is also believed that there are fierce battles between conservative and liberal believers as to the interpretation of so many issues of American history and what should actually be taught and covered in school syllabuses.

It is therefore vital for governments at all levels to get involved and try to address these issues together with the population otherwise there will be fewer and fewer people who will be in the position to defend these American values in the future especially the benefits and superiority of the free market economic system. Some of the suggested answers to the younger generations' issues include the following:

1. To increase awareness in schools and higher institutions about American history, the American way of life, the economic systems and so many other related issues, the media should also help and hold discussions by various groups and people including the young about all these matters. The young generation should also know such elementary information such as the National Anthem the main basic parts and concepts of the Constitution, the number of states and their capitals, state governors, etc. They should also know their President, the Secretaries, Members of Congress especially their local representatives. They should know about the Supreme Court judges and their tenure. They should learn about political systems of government etc. These are just examples as the list of options is endless and interesting. This can also be done through civics lessons at all levels of learning.

2. Government should create an activity for the young generation in order to remove boredom, reduce unemployment among

the young and make them participate in the affairs of their country. The government should include in their policies about job opportunities for the younger generation. They should also provide easily accessible venture capital in order to put into reality the business ideas that the young generation might have to show. These are but a few examples of what can be done.

In short, it is important to make the young generation to be part of the system they are supposed to belong to and uphold. The government should realize that the socialist philosophy of equality and resource sharing is very appealing to many people who feel they have been left out of the system. The socialist and communist systems do not encourage production and innovation. Whether one works or not they are entitled to share equally what has been produced. It takes people time to realize that the pie being shared is no more. This is because other systems do not encourage production and innovations so that what is consumed is replenished. They should therefore promote ideas and programs for self-reliance.

This is because the socialist system is not designed to fully replenish the pie. The pie keeps getting smaller and smaller and people gradually start getting more and more desperate as their shares diminish. In the end, they blame the free market forces for economic sabotage. The Leaders mobilize the people to fight this sabotage and fight for the noble cause of sharing what is no longer there. When people start to talk about the problems, they are imprisoned and purged for making anti-people statements and for crimes against the people and the state. Meanwhile, the people's general standards keep getting lower and lower except for the bosses who maintain high standards which are sometimes higher than their capitalist counterparts.

People then started regretting having shunned the free market system and democracy where at least there was assured freedom of expression and opportunity to succeed for everybody. Capitalism encourages opportunity for everybody. For instance, if everyone is given a million dollars as startup capital, by the end of 5 years the situation will be interesting to observe. Some will decide to enjoy themselves and spend their money. Others will invest it while others will trade with it and at the end of 5 years, all of them will not be equal. However what is important that all of them will be happy and free to do what they want with their money. They will have had equal opportunity. Most of all they will do this in an atmosphere that allows them to have liberty and pursuit of happiness.

There is a misunderstanding especially as portrayed by the extreme socialist philosophy that the capitalist system does not care for the common interests of society. Unfortunately, some extreme right-wing capitalist advocates tend to portray and make it appear as if this is the case. The question of providing common services is one of the main reasons for the justification of having a government. The government is supposed to provide common services for those areas where it is mutually more beneficial for the people instead of them providing such services as individuals whether capitalist or socialist the government's duty is to provide these services. This is why people pay all sorts of taxes to the government. The main areas for government to provide common services to the community for service such as security both external and internal, keep law and order, making laws in accordance with the constitution, provide social services such as schools and health care, etc. These are services which people prefer to do as a group and not as individuals. The extent to which the governments provide these services as public service or through the private sector is the question on which many opinions vary. For instance, soldiers can best serve society by serving as public servants but makers of warplanes, defense equipment, medicines, etc. is best done by the private sector.

The difference between the two systems is that under the socialist system the states or countries want to make almost all the decisions for the people. As an individual, you have little choice to make. They think they know best how people should invest, eat, sleep, raise families, occupation choices and placements, etc. People have no right to question or give their opinions. The government takes almost all you make in order to provide. The government almost controls your life.

On the other hand, the capitalist system allows you to shape your destiny other than for the services people want to share with others. These common services can still be performed by the private sector. Where the capitalist system governments differ is that the people through their representatives' vote on which services are to be done as a society other than individuals. This is the one million dollar question facing the USA today. In the USA some are of the opinion that health care should be part of the common services while others say hell no. In my case, I strongly support Universal Health Care as the answer to people's healthcare problems. Healthcare does not need to be run by public sectors but can be contracted to private sectors by the states or federal governments from the funds collected as earlier collected.

Finally, I have written this book with a positive attitude and I would pray that many people would come with more ideas on how to solve America's problems. Those who disagree with me should come out and defend their ideas of solutions rather than criticism. That's why I have made the title of this book SOLUTIONS AMERICA.

All the problems we have addressed should have been dealt with yesterday and it is therefore vital that they are attended today rather than postpone them to a later date.

History may judge us as not having been serious with the future of America. Whether Republican, Democrat or independent it is important to collectively address these issues together now.

END

JOHN NDEGE

BORN JULY 12 1946
Married with children
Diploma in Banking—Institute of Bankers 1969
Banker 1967-1980 Grindlays Bank—Officer Trainee Bank
Manager, Country Operations and planning manager
Parliamentary Candidate UPM Party ticket (unsuccessful) 1980
Uganda controversial Elections
Kenya—exile owner Kibichiku Hotel 1980-1985
A businessman from 1981 to date
Ministry of rehabilitation—coordinator food relief Luwero
triangle, and North Uganda war-affected zones 1986 to 1988
Chairman Grain Exporters Association up to 2001
Vice-Chairman Eastern Uganda National Chamber of Commerce
1999 up to 2001
Hon. Member of Uganda Parliament 1989-2001
Hon. Member Parliamentary Standing Committee Finance and
Planning 1997-2001
Chairman Finance and Planning Committee 2000 - 2001
Chairman Parliamentary Standing Committee and Members
Privileges 1991 - 1997
Delegate to Constitution-making Assembly for Uganda 1990-1995
Been resident in the USA from 2001 to date
The Author of Solution America

Lightning Source UK Ltd.
Milton Keynes UK
UKHW011933060821
388460UK00001B/49